LOVERS

LOVERS

CHELSIE DIANE

POEMS AND POWER

LOVERS © 2024 Chelsie Diane.

All rights reserved. This book or any portion thereof may not be reproduced or used in any manner whatsoever without the express written permission of the publisher except for the use of brief quotations in a book review. For information, please contact the publisher.

ISBN: 979-8-9862272-1-4

Cover art and photographer: Peter Kagan

Cover graphic artist: Heidi Green

Copy editor: Mindy Laks

Book design & layout: Josie and Sophie Bassett. twooaksdesign.co

First printing edition, 2024.

Chelsie Diane
www.chelsiediane.com
@poemsandpeonies

for my best lover.

the bravest
the worst of them all
the truest of the true
chelsie diane.

there's a man who's been out sailing
in a decade full of dreams
and he takes her to a schooner
and he treats her like a queen
bearing beads from california
with their amber stones and green
he has called her from the harbor
he has kissed her with his freedom
he has heard her off to starboard
in the breaking and the breathing
of the water weeds
while she was busy being free
there's a man who's climbed a mountain
and he's calling out her name
and he hopes her heart can hear three thousand miles
he calls again
he can think her there beside him
he can miss her just the same
he has missed her in the forest
while he showed her all the flowers
and the branches sang the chorus
as he climbed the scaley towers
of a forest tree
while she was somewhere being free
there's a man who's sent a letter
and he's waiting for reply
he has asked her of her travels
since the day they said goodbye
he writes "wish you were beside me
we can make it if we try"
he has seen her at the office
with her name on all his papers
through the sharing of the profits
he will find it hard to shake her
from his memory
and she's so busy being free
there's a lady in the city
and she thinks she loves them all
there's the one who's thinking of her
there's the one who sometimes calls
there's the one who writes her letters
with his facts and figures scrawl
she has brought them to her senses
they have laughed inside her laughter
now she rallies her defenses
for she fears that one will ask her
for eternity
and she's so busy being free
there's a man who sends her medals
he is bleeding from the war
there's a jouster and a jester and a man who owns a
store
there's a drummer and a dreamer
and you know there may be more
she will love them when she sees them
they will lose her if they follow
and she only means to please them
and her heart is full and hollow
like a cactus tree
while she's so busy being free

joni mitchell

poems and short stories

every lover i've ever had shows up at my funeral

i once called her a bitch
and she ripped the cognac glass out of my hand
raised it above her head. shattered it.
remembered my daughter.
her bare feet
silently swept
and drove away forever.

she told me i bored her
she told me she was a mermaid that had swallowed a dragon
she told me if i had a feather i could fly
she told me i was sorely mistaken about chemtrails and god
she told me her angels said i was a liar

i painted her naked
and when she fell asleep i covered her
put her poetry book in her hands

i am the sad poet.
no that's me!
no that's me!
she called me her pretty little boy
she called me her war crime
she called me her cowboy lucifer
she went to my gallery opening night
and told me it was full of demons
she vomited in my porsche

she moved to mexico to marry me
i told her i didn't believe in magic
and when i said i needed time
she told me she didn't believe in time.

i married her for ten years.
she told me she was building our nest
she built a launch pad.

best sex of my life. we died!
best sex of my life. i saw my past life as her servant boy
best sex of my life. i told her i loved her date three.
date four. date two.
my mother still asks about her.
she wrote an entire poem about my hands.

i am the woman of the poems
her magnet. her mistake. her cowgirl.
i'm entirely insane and she tackled me for it.
tied me by my wrists
broke me out of a columbian prison.

i am jeanne pierre
i smoked a cigarette naked at the window
in marie antoinette's bedroom
she said you look like peter pan
she was always peter pan.

i was her guitar teacher.
i went down on her
and then she asked me to leave.

i am the spartan waiter
i slapped her in bed and
she punched me in the face!

she was delusional!
delusional! delusional!
every lover i've ever had shows up at my funeral
bitter and silvered and bruised
with wet paint on their hands

and
still
irrevocably
and
madly
in love with me.

HER

The first time I saw her, it was one a.m. in a jungle in Columbia. I was four hours down a dirt road from Bogota. I smelled like the Tico that picked me up and drove me in his silver 1993 Nissan through the jungle. Hell, I looked like him now too. His car was a tin can, the seats covered in dirt, windows down the whole way, the air thick enough to smear. My stomach was sharp and nauseous. I had been horseback in a thunderstorm for days. The potholes had cracked my cervical spine like hairlines in concrete.

We pulled up the hill to the jungle cabins and got stuck four times. Every time, Santiago cussed in Spanish and motioned me to get out in the mud and help him push. When we rolled up, my legs were dipped in mud. She stood there a mountain. She stood there a snake. She stood there my boy and Athena with Medusa's head on her shield. She stood there like an embryo stuck inside her wet jungle mama. A jungle mama doesn't play by the rules. You drink her root and die. In the jungle there is more than one moon. In the jungle everything you see could kill you. In the jungle there are jaguars that will wake you with their yellow eyes. And in the jungle, every time, it will be the last thing you ever see.

Howler monkeys bellowed like a pack of mean dogs in the sky. I, too, was in a uterus. A baby canaled, waiting to be born in caul. The mother wasn't thinking about her placenta. No. We were growing from her cord without a thought from her. Ovid's metamorphosis. Omphale with Hercules in chains dressing him as her little girl. Like Rimbauld, I had disappeared to Africa on a ship that would never come home.

I knew inexplicably and suddenly I was madly in love with her.
She had the male gaze I didn't expect and I thought of my escaped beauty on that drive that had climbed out the window up a tree four hours away. I was aware of the zit I picked on my chin in the cab, the deep pores in my nose, the mud stuck to my ankles. My body was bruised from the ride. I smelled like Santiago. Our hair drank the same smoke. I tried to dip into my chest hiding my country birth, hiding my defects. You could scrape the tired from my neck.

She stood under the covered hallway wrapped in the blanket of Jacob's ladder, wrapped in a sonata. She wasn't what I thought. She was a bible character. She was the husband I lost to the war. My under-brain did not say hello to a woman or a friend. When I finally spoke, I said hello to a lover.

All the moving things and music gathered in me at once. All the wood in the cave of me, burning. I could feel the forgotten things again. Stuff in me like jazz and old tied off wrists. I fumbled my carry-on and it fell into the mud. She was nervous. She was bouncing up on her toes. She was smiling like a fucking idiot.

I walked toward her biting the inside of my cheek. I thought I should kiss her. I thought I should pump my veins with heroine and die curled between her legs in some club bathroom. I thought I should cut off my arm lest it make me sin. DEAR JESUS PLUCKETH MYNE OWN EYES. Why the hell did I almost kiss her? I am not gay. I am her mother. I was 32. She was 25. Extreme. Sharp. Fluorescent like a nineties song. Audrey Hepburn in Rome with a cigarette when she married the psychiatrist and told the press to fuck off. I wanted to suck the corners of her song. Gnaw her hips. Chew her like jerky.

We followed each other online. She was brave and I liked watching her move. The month before I showed up in the jungle in the middle of the night she had called me. She made some comment online like an idiot about women being women! Men being men! The trans community ate her alive. The comments were sick. The world was canceling her for her stupidity. The girl was not dumb, but she was dumb. She didn't even believe what she typed. No one looked more like a pretty boy than her. She was the crowned king of taking everything too far. When she called, I thought she was going to kill herself publicly or kill someone else. I had never met her. I loved her because she was brave and stupid. No, she was stupid brave. I loved her because there was no in between. I called her and told her to shut the fuck up. "Why do you care what they do? What do you know about shit? You're 25!" I asked her what was beneath it. "Are you gay? We're all gay! What kind of bullshit christian narrative are you publicly purging from your childhood? Stop. It's ugly. You have no dog in this fight."

She didn't even want a fight. All the dogs she ever adopted she gave to her mother after a week. No. She wanted to scream off a canyon, clear her throat and side with some kind of new age community so they would love her like the church didn't. She apologized publicly and called me minutes later. She decided to fly to the jungle and do ayahuasca. She wanted to kill what was killing her.

The next week during her ceremony, she called me in the middle of the night. *Why the hell am I her call?* I had never met this woman. I had talked to her once. I knew she was freaking out. I could feel her fear pulsing through my own lungs. I purposely didn't answer. I turned my phone off and tossed it from me. Buck up buttercup. Eat the mother and die. I believed in her too much to answer. I know now it was the part of me that wanted her to get ready enough for me. Puke out your bullshit!

Subconsciously, I was asking her to make me a room, to put a pretty pillow in the middle of the bed for me.

I called her the next morning and told her I had a week without my kids. I wanted her to say, come. She said come. She was teaching yoga at a retreat center where she stayed for free. She was always escaping, a thief on the run. This time NYC, a Puerto Rican asshole, some older man, who wanted her as we all wanted her and wanted her always chasing him. Wanting her and...

And is not how this woman works. I know this because it ain't how I work either.

"Come here. Come. Chelsie, come. Please!"

She sent me a Garth Brooks song. She was sex. She was a chiseled David. She was a shadow machine. She was already my worst mistake; a white flame cold. When I saw her, I froze. We hugged, my mouth in her neck, longing to lick her hot milk like a kitten. I wanted to lick her dick. I almost bit her. I was a boy. She was a boy. My tits were talking. Her hips were talking. Her ass. Her fucking ass. Oh God, she was still going home to her mother. I was a mother! I wanted to kiss her so badly, I could barely breathe. My teeth were standing edged. My teeth were on a cliff in the wind. My teeth were stacked white wants.

She had saved me a plate of dinner. She watched me eat. The woman was everything I was afraid of, the black water rolling on the floor of the deepest ocean. She was what you drink only after you drown. She was touching her neck with one hand. The other had an invisible energetic feather she was tracing my bare body with, leaning back in her chair watching me eat. She was the most beautiful human I had ever seen. Her skin was wet gold. It was as if God had just sent her down putting all her favorite touches on. I couldn't stand it. I reached under the table and touched her leg with my toe. She flushed and pushed her seat back.

"Get the fuck away from me! Chelsie, godammit," she said, smiling from ear to ear.

"Sorry. I'm confused because I want you and I am not gay! I am not gay!"

"I'm not gay either!"

My head was swollen, spinning, a celestial body. I backed up my chair. I was dizzy and younger. I had forgotten how to think like a divorced mother. I was a crushed out 14 year old, Pete Grawson after school putting half his granola bar in his mouth asking me to take the other half. I was a quick asteroid about to hit.

There was something pulling on my lower neck. There was something sucking the blood at my wrists. My clit was swollen. I was growing a cock that would not stop swelling. The red thing between us sunk it's fingernails into our eyes and yelled, "I'm going to wake you the fuck up and its going to hurt like hell." Both of us could hear it. Both of us thought we could outsmart it. Trick it. Tie it to a jungle tree and refuse it, leave it until we could interrogate it. Starve it.

We stood across the dining room from each other staring. My heart was cut out with a dull knife and was sinking into a mayan cenote. "Let's go swimming," she said.

I put on my red bikini and I dove in. She wore yellow tiny triangles. She was the strongest body I had ever seen. I wanted her in the back of my daddy's truck on a country road. I wanted her thick thighs. I wanted her straddling me. I wanted to bite her collarbones and choke her. I wanted to roll her and roll her and roll her. I wanted to pin her down by her wrists and lick up her mandible. God, I was a horny man.

I'm not gay. I needed to sleep. What jungle parasite had crawled into my brain and mushed it gay?

I had to go to bed. Eight hours and this desire will be pushed from my brain. She swam toward me. It was two a.m. The jungle was loud. "You get the fuck away from me!" I said smiling this time in the moonlight.

I pushed her hard. Too hard to be playful.

We stood on opposite sides of the pool. She bit her cheek, smiling.

"What's going on?" I asked, tilting my head.

"What's going on Chelsie Diane?" She tilted her head too.

"Fuck," I said.

"Fuck!" she said.

"Goodnight girl," I spoke as I climbed out wet.

Walking through the dark jungle to my hut, I didn't look back. I had to get to sleep so I could wake from her. But I knew that as soon as I did she was going to knock on my cabin door. I had just fallen asleep. The rain was beating on the roof of the tin like the thousand tiny fists of god. Then, her fist. I ran to open.

Our bodies hit and didn't stop hitting. Warm and knotted and humid and fighting like two wrestlers. A swarm of tongue and hands and kidney and throat. My hands and ass and her hands and my hands pulling back her thick aubrey bob. Her moan. She grabbed me by the neck and vampired my collarbones slowing us down.

The force between us toppled us, messed the bed to our knees. She was stronger than me. She rolled on top of me and straddled me and kissed my eyelids, my earlobe, pulled my hair with her teeth. I fisted the sheets as she drank my entire body and I hers and we arched and arched and arched. The cock of the universe entered both of us and fucked us to god simultaneously. She screamed. We shook and shook. I had to hold her down several times while she quaked, our legs locked, covered in sweat, all the sheets thrown off the cabin bed until we held each other and cried. Then we wanted more and started slithering again for it. She spoke in tongues while she hummed. It sent me over the edge of the bed as I attempted to hold on to her shoulder. My leg kept her tied to our earth…to our human birth.

"Making love to you," I said, broken humming, "is making love to myself."

"Chelsie, when does this stop for women?" she asked at 6am.

I slapped her clay smoothed yoga flank. We were weak, soaking wet, our knees sore from shaking.

"When does *this* stop?"

"We have to decide to stop."

"We're heroin addicts. We need sponsors."

"We have to make up our minds about this and we have to make this stop," she said.

When we tried, our hands shook. More. I pulled her sweaty face from mine and held her three inches from my eyes; the locked eye portal to hell. The insatiable spit. The bad desire. The burning. The bible.

The next morning we were so quiet. When I held her waking body, I could hear her thoughts.

"Chelsie? I hate that I feel like this. I feel so guilty. Does God hate us?"

"The god that hates this, I hate," I said.

"Me too."

I pressed my chest to hers. The something that came down and fucked us the night before scrambled and was hiding again like it had our whole lives.

We held hands up the jungle hill for breakfast. Halfway up, without a word, we let go, nodded to each other and she walked ahead. We didn't have to say anything. The people at the resort were families. They employed her. Our touch profane. It would be different if I was a man; the interest, the hope they would have for our romance. The old men that owned the place would wink. Their eyes would throw parties for our coming.

But we were women.

Our heads understood these things. Our hands though, only hearts in those. When they dropped to the jungle floor, they were suddenly so empty. We still hadn't yet made it to the life that loved our love. We walked in silence. She was a few steps ahead of me. The clouds were ripping. The jungle was yelling her birthing cries.

It would not stop raining for weeks.

~

Later that summer, she faked her covid test because, "fuck the government," she said, forgetting she had to have a QR code and was arrested at the airport. I had to break her out of a Columbian prison. She was Hunter S. Thompson stumbling into walls being escorted out in handcuffs, breaking a glass bottle as they carried her out screaming, "FUCK ALL OF YOU BASTARDS!" She hated rules. Broke them all just to watch them break and believed every conspiracy about the government and was planning on revoking her citizenship and sending her birth certificate back to the Vatican. And I loved her for it all.

But there were things I was beginning to hate. Like how she had bought the same dress and started using my exact lines writing them in poems as her own. I hated the feeling of being slowly erased. It wasn't her fault. She was mad. Not mad to live. Mad to feel, which is dangerous. She was young, penetrable, like a veil. Everything in me could be seen through her.

When I was twenty-five, I was still married, had baby girl twins and no thoughts of leaving. I was still attending church twice on Sundays. How could I expect her twenty-five to be muscled enough to climb out of illusion into her full skin? She was cocooned. It was dark and wet and there were no signs of wings. I thought I knew when she'd emerge. But I remember as an eight year old, keeping nine cocoons in a jar and waiting all winter. I remember how only two made it out. The others stayed sleeping. Still, they are somewhere sleeping. The two went to the sky, the rest went to earth. None of them were mine. I knew she couldn't be mine. I loved her as much as I hated her for it.

I started not talking freely, thinking if I say this she will peel it out of my hands. It was like I was hiding my jewelry from a thief. I started over the top encouraging her in everything that was purely her and not me. Yes, get your eyebrow pierced! Yes! Start a band! Yes, get your next level yoga certification! She trusted me and I felt like a fucking asshole for my reasoning. I wanted her to be hers so she could be mine. I used half of my days trying to decipher what was hers and to hold it in front of her like a precious jewel so she would swallow it. I had three children and was in a divorce. It was like being in a lion's den surrounded by lions only I could see. She thought we were in Columbia at a mud massage. At an acai bowl place. At a yoga class.

I was in a lion's den.
She was in a black cocoon.
I was losing sleep, my hours, my peace.

She was never insane to me. She was only always truly great. There is a difference. She was twenty-five years old and greater than anyone I had known. With her, I felt more myself than I had ever felt with a man. She knew me. She just didn't know that I was drowning. She loved me so much and was penetrable. If she was around me longer than a few hours, she'd start looking like me. It's not a chameleon's fault they change the color of the branch. And I wasn't a branch unless that branch was in a hurricane. Spinning, spinning, and knowing it would never land on earth again.

She came to town last week after four years. It will never leave. She's different now. A musician. She is her own maybe. Three years of psychosis and chain breaking. She drank the medicine and castrated the demons and, from what she tells me, she has won. She drove to Malibu and kissed me in front of everyone at Soho House who before figured I was straight. She loved that shit. She came home with me. We swigged red wine on my kitchen floor straight out of the bottle and were tangled and naked for days.

She took a photo of my hands.

I took her to a cowboy bar and fed her a bloody steak.

To this day, she thinks I had her arrested in Columbia because she left me.
This would be a great place to tell you if I did. But I did not.

The truth is, as much as I screamed at her for turning with her suitcase that day to leave me, as much as I was begging her to stay, I wanted her gone. When she walked out that morning to fly to a another country she would not stay, I found a scorpion climbing up my cabin wall. I put her in a jar and freed her in the jungle. But right before I did, I took off the lid and watched her crawl up the side of the jar slowly toward me. Something in me that no one but the poets understand wanted to keep a thing that dangerous climbing up my wall
wanted to fall asleep once more
knowing something so close
had the power to kill me.

i call to say
we have no other choice
but to date for a year
go our separate ways
and cheat on whoever we're with forever
i call to say we're fucked bertha.
it's too late now
we must now enter the study with jim carrey
cauterize our frontal lobe memories
me because i'm three million years old and riding a pterodactyl
you because you found the plug to my pool
and the grass in the yard grew
me because i'm sick of your shit.
anyway we've always been
the mermaids drowning men
no shells on our tits
me because when i was a kid
a cow ate nightshade and dropped over dead
you because i went looking for it
go do a thousand doses of ayahuasca!
beg for another cup of thick root
puke up your gallbladder soot.
i call you to tell you about the half spined men
under my feet
and clean my bloodied beak
we should date the worms we eat?
i call you to say there are transparent octopi
and ya let's just be friends.
i'll cry in bed with him

and you'll
shave your fucking head
again

i am doing everything i can to stay sitting.
some line in french.
some line in tongues.
some line in my ten year old voice
telling you to come home.
i watch you watch an opera.
you come in and sit in the corner in something very blue
that has little tears that i can not sew.
you've been chewing the skin on your thumb.
the violin makes me sick.
i hold you in the bottom of my jaw.
i hold your naked back arched and wet.
your neck takes a room in my rotting back tooth.
the bow has become a sea of wild bees.
my bottom lip is tripping through
the dark air
i am afraid to get to you.
tu me manques.
(you are missing from me)
and not this minute
not this minute
but i will leave the theater.
knowing the weight to stand from velvet-
to pull from those ox yoked-
is the lie that makes our backs bend old
why. must. i. go.
in the ways they say?
a man will pull up my carriage.
he will have no face.
do you hear me?
none of them will.

what i'm saying is that you are a whirling dervish
you eagle of the totem pole
you astral plane
you the starry night
and the bit off ear
what i'm saying is i say your name
and learn the whisp whisp of the jazz drum
what i'm saying is your name can not be written in pencil
your name requires a chisel stone
you are the hail mary
the buzzer beater
the jamoa al norte cliff
no running start.
no running start.
you jump.
what i'm saying is
god gave me a mouth the size of jupiter
what i'm saying is i am mic jagger
and steven tyler's baby
what i'm saying is
i could eat you.
what i'm saying is
a prayer
that our teeth rot from our heads!
what i'm saying is we know they will anyway
and open our pretty mouths
what i'm saying is your neck makes me
break into the asshole of the sphinx and steal
a jade scarab beetle
from the tomb of osiris
what i'm saying is let's free britney
duck through the lasers
tape her father to a chair
take her to tamarindo
get her off lithium
and hear her low voice return
what i'm saying is i will bring you a flower for your hair
and one for britney too.
and then meet elon

and tell him to ship us to the hottest ray of the sun
what i'm saying is any ship with us on it
would run out of fuel on national tv
what i'm saying is
they will all watch us
drive
straight
into
the
sun

there is a holy man
from an african tribe near timbuktu
that will spend his entire life
sitting outside a cave
protecting seven hundred year old drawings
these drawings predicted seven centuries before us
the rotation of sirius b
the white dwarf planet was the heaviest in the world
(1.5 million tons per cubic inch!)
the helium carbon process of star death
of pulsars and magnetars
and the hydrogen cloud womb of baby stars
the lymphatic drainage of our disease
the oxygenation map of your bluest cell
you love me
and i order ten books on the incas
become fluent in sanskrit
catch the next flight to cusco
curse every man god
bow to flat drawings of the dolphins of the dogons
you love me
and i circle two hundred times per minute into a supernova
and ten million galaxies are birthed from the explosion
you love me
and i spend the rest of my life
at the entrance of the oldest cave on earth
knowing that every question
every scientist has squinted into
every microscope for
is painted
behind me.

ROCK

We were babies.
This is the only thing you will get about him.
It's what I tell my children when they ask.

Thirteen years ago when I was married and had seven month old twins, we went on a vacation with his family to St. Armands. We rented a house on a peninsula. The yard was surrounded by ocean on three sides. No beach, just grass, a concrete fence, then a sea. At the end there was a small dock, a sailboat tarped and tied.

One night, I used the wrong cleaner on the counter tops and my mother in law was really upset. "These countertops are granite!" she cried. The sailboat was framed in the window behind her and suddenly, I remembered my legs. When she was finished, I put down the rag and walked to the dock, unzipped the tarp and laid down in the boat.

Hours passed.
My babies were sleeping.
I had quit medical school. I had stopped teaching. And worse, I had stopped writing. I married a man that loved me–perhaps in his way–but I was not seen or heard. So I became a quiet song.

There are numerous studies surrounding why some birds stop singing. I know why.

Nobody came outside to look for me. They went to bed. I remember watching the house lights quietly turn off, one by one. My own husband went to bed without me. My tears could have written a poem a thousand miles long, just to live inside.

After a while, the sailboat rocked me to sleep. I woke up in the middle of the night to a pod of dolphins whistling and clicking outside the boat. They were rocking the boat with their noses. I put my arm over the side and they swam to me and did tricks and played and flipped up and out of the water and swam directly to my reaching arm to nose my hand. This happened for an hour or so and I knew suddenly and wonderfully and horribly that I was more known, more loved in a night ocean than I was inside my life.

I leaned over the edge and cheered and laughed and played and I sang.

The next morning early, I walked back inside and made breakfast and nobody asked, so I never told. But I thought of it often when I was lonely. And I was lonely often.

I'm not religious, but there is something Jesus said that I can not shake, *if you don't love me. Even the rocks will cry out!*

Maybe love is always reaching for us.
Maybe it's us that have forgotten our legs, forgotten the dolphins, forgotten that if another can not love us, if we listen,
even the rocks will cry out.

my daughter tells my ex husband
"that's mommy's favorite song!"
his new wife is in the car
he turns it off.
praise the lord
you can't listen to dolly
without thinking of me.

you know the day i taught you
how to back the tractor out of the hay barn
the chicken coop needed moved
you lifted it in the air
look at you city boy!

my mother made us sleep in different rooms
i snuck down the creaking hall at 2 am
we had bought a kama sutra book red faced
i made you learn every line.
you were a blue eyed baby
your daddy kept volunteering for the war
mine kept putting me in one
two prisoners of war
that found a key
there's no way i was getting out of there without you
twelve years
i knew what i owed
i put her in your life like a thumb tacked paper doll
i was so careful
folding her paper hooks around you
when her husband left her i showed up
with a casserole
held the three day old baby you would adopt
kissed her cheek
said you're going to be ok honey.
and slipped out the back door
telling you where to go.
i always said you were
good with directions
so sure never lost

but the thing we both know
about dolly
is you can turn her off
but she's always
still singing
somewhere.

MOHAVE

I once drove six hours to the desert with two-hundred and fifty-three poems to seek closure from the only man I had ever fallen in love with. I rented an airbnb cabin in the middle of the desert several miles down dirt tracks. *Turn left at the Jesus cactus with arms*, the directions said.

When I arrived late, I realized I had booked a guest house owned by an elderly woman. She left on the light and stayed up to explain the tea kettle and I told her my plan.

"I have to know. I can't live anymore not knowing," I told her.

"I know honey." I showed her photos of my kids. "I know honey," she said, again.

When I walked into the cafe and he saw me from the kitchen, he dropped a plate and it shattered. He stood looking at me exactly how I had imagined he would. His hair was longer. His jaw, thinner. His skin tanned by the desert. He was still him. He was still mine.

"It's the girl," he said.

"The girl from Kansas City?" I heard the dishwasher ask, "*That* girl?!'

~

He stuck a stick of nag champa in his car air vent. I pointed at it, "won't this catch your car on fire?"
He didn't answer.

He was sleeping on the floor in a concrete box. There were no windows. His entire place was the size of my bathroom. There were a few pillows he found at Goodwill. He said he was used to this from when he lived in India. I was sweaty and shaky and kept complimenting everything from a world I had never known; a Buddhist book, palo santo, a pair of black jeans hanging over a plastic sink, and a tiny pre-lit tree he used for a lamp that his mother sent him. "I can't believe you're here. You're crazy Chelsie Diane. Are the kids with him? He still hates me?"

"Yes."

I don't remember a time when I had been hugged like that, such small arms to cover an entire belief system of a whole woman. Yet, I wasn't a woman. And I definitely wasn't whole. I was suddenly both my first cell and last living mitochondria and could remember novas and the reef, that I was going to die someday and would name the thousands being born. Touching him I was something new, we were the beginning and the end, the alpha and the omega, no middle in sight.

Everything was doomed.
There were no choices here.

If you had a choice in your love, I'm not saying it's not love. I'm just saying it's not the love that we had.

There was only one piece of art leaning against the concrete wall. He painted on a piece of cardboard. It was us in New York City in the rain kissing beneath an umbrella.

We never had an umbrella.

I walked over to it and held it. "I'm taking this home,"

I remembered our homes were different homes.

Horrible.

I wanted to take him with me, shave him, feed him, bathe him, anoint him with oil and kiss his forehead.

He was struggling again, paranoid. He told me he spent hours meditating, about how sometimes he didn't see another human for weeks, that he wasn't calling his mother back. He told me of the peyote journey where he almost froze to death.

When my diamond lightning bolt earring fell out in the desert, I did not look for it. I pointed at the wolf, the unmoving pillar of salt staring at us. *Please don't read into this, please god.* He said his phone broke when she texted him, that he had dropped it and it shattered– surely a sign of her darkness. He was partying with artists that lived in

RVs and one night, a woman had crawled in bed with him. I couldn't hear any of it after he said her name. My mind was predatory toward my heart, a starving animal that smelled poisoned meat. *Did he fuck her?* I was green. Never before have I wanted to be something I would hate to be. But I wanted to be childless, uneducated, broke and hate myself. I wanted to apply for waitressing jobs in the desert in vintage leather that smelled like his blunt. I wanted his cruel superstitions. I wanted a drug in my vein that could numb him.

"I have to get surgery next week. I'm in pain," I told him. *Check on me. I'm scared,* I didn't say.

I regretted telling him. I wished I was a moth; the papery thin one you could see through, something that could live in the dark in a concrete box, that could feed on the compost in his paper bag, born without a mouth to only live a day.

He wanted space, he said. He wasn't used to this. This is a lot. He got in the shower.

"I should go," I tried to read his face.

"No, it's fine," he mumbled.

His journal was laying on the floor. I checked the cracked door. The shower was on. I'd be ok as long as I could hear it. I had to.

Don't you dare say you wouldn't.
You don't know.

It was the journal you find after someone disappears.

I read quickly. On page one he had written, *I hate myself.* The shower was loud. The door cracked. I kept looking up wondering if there was a mirror. He wrote the name of his ex wife in different fonts. *Shame.* He wrote the word shame. *Sorry.* He was sorry about me. A flurry of black lines so dark it punctured the page. There was nowhere to go from here. He said it. He wrote he was cursed for loving me. There was not a single word about wanting me. I was the witch that poisoned the well. I was the temptress; Lilith in the tree with sharpened teeth. My spine twitched and I could no longer remember how to cut a tomato.

Something in me said, *go*. There were currents pulsing into my eyes. I thought I may pass out. *Get in your jeep and dust this desert road and go*. But I had gifts. The old woman from the airbnb made jewelry and I had commissioned a rosary made for him out of turquoise. I bought him a warmer blanket, a two hundred year old handmade piece that was supposedly used by Native Americans. It was all selfish. I wanted him adorned in memory. I wanted him covered in me.

When he came out I was hunched over the counter making cashew cheese. I didn't fucking know how to make cashew cheese. He sat on the floor behind me where he couldn't see me rotting. The dinner was shit. I have no idea what it was. I lied that it was vegan. We sat on the concrete floor. A cold floor. A floor like a dog kennel. A floor made so you could hose the piss down the drain. I couldn't eat. He finished his plate, then mine too. I turned to him. "You have to kiss me. Goddammit, kiss me." I was about to claw out of my cage bone. He leaned close to my face where I could feel the heat of his mouth but then stopped.

"Chelsie, do you think that's a good idea?"

There were tears in his eyes, too. I couldn't answer. *I could make you want to live again*, I almost said. *Let me*, I almost said. *Suck my soul again. I give consent. Suck it with your next breath like the mermaids song. Turn me into dry ground. Turn me into this desert.*

He slowly moved his head side to side yet slightly toward me. Slowly, no. He couldn't stop moving slightly towards me. I didn't dare move. He stilled. All I had to do was lean one millimeter more. We both knew it. If I made love to him, I loved him more than I loved myself.

When I took his cock into my throat, he arched over and kissed my spine.

"I hate every woman you love," I said after.

"Really? I'd be happy to see you happy?"

"Don't say that," I said. "I hate that."

He rolled the other way. It wasn't my fault and it wasn't his but I didn't know that then.

"Are you sleeping here?" he asked.

All I heard was get up and drive away.

This is the last time. I promised myself.
I didn't sleep. I watched him. No, I memorized him.

I drove away at sunrise screaming, beating the steering wheel with my fists. The woman from the airbnb was on the porch, as if waiting for me to arrive. I couldn't speak, just shook my swollen head, mascara ash trailed my cheeks. She took me to her room. "Oh sweetie," she said. "I knew how this would go."

I cried face down on her bed.

"Get it all out honey." This woman, this stranger, rubbed my back while my reddest organ split onto her bed, circling my back with her old hands. "I know. I really do know because I was also married to a doctor, had three children and fell in love with a man that was completely unavailable. I held on and it almost killed me. It took all the life from me trying to stay. I could feel him moving away from me every second. It was horrible honey. Mine was married. Mine was Jeff Bridges."

I shot up from the bed.

"You were in love with Jeff Bridges?!"

"Yes, the charismatic little fucker about killed me."

"How does our story end?" I asked.

"You love yourself enough to close the door, honey. The kids grow up. Two in NorCal, one in LA. Your son gets published by a small agency in the Bay. It pisses his dad off that he doesn't become a doctor. You never regret leaving. That man didn't love you. Your daughter calls you every day. You meet a man in a honky tonk, your true love. You buy this house in the desert. Every day you hike this mountain. You grow old together. He knows you'll need a way to make money. He builds this little Airbnb. He died three years ago. You miss him terribly, terribly every day."

She was crying now.

I drove home with a tupperware full of soup, wrapped in a dishcloth. A few weeks later, I got hernia surgery. Drunk on pain meds and laying in bed, I got a call from a number I didn't recognize. "How are you doing my love?"

It's not him, never is.

It's her.

do you know what an inoculum is?
a grave digging tool
a cormorant's dive
the hypnotist snaps. no one wakes.
the coal cart is empty and going back in
the first man that touches me after you.

he breathes on me and i am stolen land
i crawl into my own ventricles
he asks are you ok?
i say keep going.
what i mean is the storm is outside the house
what i mean is windows are breaking
what i mean is i am in four walled compartments
what i mean is i am so deep in my own red
and the blood is loud
if i screamed he could not hear me here
what i mean is this new man will touch me
without ever touching me
what i mean is
he is trespassing
what i mean is guillotine!
what i mean is the nucleus adulterated
what i mean is there are chambers that backflow
what i mean is you still live here.
you still live here.
what i mean is my body has become the temple of doom
setting traps for his limb
what i mean is
his hands move up my thigh
i must keep him from falling into an abyss
when his mouth is on my neck
the boulder tries to roll
he pulls back my hair
i swallow the lava
he raises my shirt
i flash a wall of throwing knives
what i mean is this new man is a good man!
a thief

a jean valjean
and took the safe without the key
and i mean
i hate him
and i mean
where are you?
and i mean
i curse
the hands
that come
after
you

LYON

On my thirty-second birthday, in the middle of my terrible divorce, I took the train to Lyon from Paris because the first man I ever fell in love with, the man from the desert, pointed to a map.

"Here. I live here even when I am not here."

I couldn't find him anymore. Right before we ruined each other's lives, he had a french wife and I had a doctor husband. It was the way cows are shot in the head for meat, how their organs melt into the field, how it grows greener in that place the next year. We were butchered and rotting making a green greener. And then like that, we were gone, in the way gone is unrecoverable, and bones are sand, the way your grandmother is gone, the way the world watched the challenger explode seconds into her flight. Nobody really knows why the challenger turned to molecules, but everyone has their theories. I bet someone as delusional as me went to the places Christa McAuliffe loved after she was skydust, believing, almost certain she would still be sitting on the stairs of the cathedral there smoking a blunt.

When I got to Lyon, I walked his steps along the river where he used to sell art as a street painter, wearing black t-shirts and black jeans and black chuck taylors and smoking the black cigarettes that he rolled. Filters in the drawer by the bed. Smoke inside every hair. Smoke on his cock, in his throat, sweet smoke that I can still taste. Smoke that I fed on, lived on years after it was gone. Smoke doing what smoke does. So much smoke it looks solid, like a wall, a mountain, something you could climb.

But no, you just walk on through.

I had to go to where I could find the pieces of the explosion, so I could taste him, climb him again. I had been crazy, he had been crazy, though in different ways. I was the wrong way to him, and he was the wrong way to me.

One night, years later, when I was laying in bed with a crazy man I would never fall in love with, I got a message from his sister about a poem she liked that I wrote online. *(I know what you're thinking: if they're all crazy, then I'm the crazy one. Fine.)* I had been lying there with him sleeping next to me deciding if I could love him. As soon as I saw her message, I decided I couldn't. More so, I promised I wouldn't.

Are you alive? Are you alive? Are your molecules in space?

I stalked her incessantly for years looking for a trace of him. They were close. Maybe I could see a photo of him married, or working on her flower farm in Maine. She didn't know me, but I knew her. Wild how that happens in this world. And now? It was like his spirit was finding me through her. Reaching right through the poems about him to his own damn sister. She could feel her own dna. Her hands in the earth with the dahlias, she could feel it.

These poems are about your brother.
My brother?!
Ya, remember the girl from Kansas City?! That's me.
Oh my god.
How is he?

She left. Ten minutes later.

How is he?

Silence.
Two days later.

How is he?

She unfollowed me.

I was a wreck. A fury. Emailing her. Checking every online newspaper in every town that felt like him for a death announcement. Was he homeless? I could feel him still living–I'd know. That's all I had to go off of–I'd know. The last time I saw him he was sleeping on a concrete floor in the Mohave. He had lost his mind but at least he was breathing.

I loved him more than any man I've ever loved. Tell him that. It was never read.

So I did what I had to do, the thing that made no sense at all. I flew to Lyon, France.

I dragged my suitcase up three hundred ancient stairs to my thousand year old apartment then walked to the art market by the river. The same one where he would sell spray painted cardboard fragments left by the homeless atop street graters. One was of us in New York City. I still have it at the top of my closet.

When I got off the train in Lyon, there was a protest happening in the streets for the working class. He would have been there dressed in all black, a blunt in one hand, sign in the other, marching.

I stopped in front of a man in all black selling his art by the river, just as he did. I bought a drawing of a woman opening a book with a flock of ravens flying to the skies.

"Because I am letting go." I told the street painter it was my thirty-first birthday. It was.

"Joyeux Anniversaire," he said in a way that made the tears roll up and burn. I walked by the river begging God to feel something again.

I looked a little too hard at the water, the Saone, and stared into the night thinking of all the ways to fake my death. *Dear lord. Please let some gorgeous French man make love to me tonight, kissing every part of my body, saying it the way he said it.*

That night, I wore black velvet and fur, like a large cat with her ass in the air. The most beautiful man, a teacher at a deaf school, walked by me as I sat at the candlelit restaurant table in the alley. I winked and told him to sit. He spoke no english. I was the deaf school. He had six roommates, so he walked up the stairs of the ancient apartment I rented with me. I told him it was my birthday. I told him to sit down on the bed and watch as I took off my velvet. What I didn't tell him was to kiss every part of my body saying Joyeux Anniversaire every time he came up for air. But he did. "Merci," I said, as he breathed heavy into my neck. "Merci. Merci." He didn't know it, but I wasn't thanking him.

I was thanking God.

I devoured him. An Aquarius. He had tattooed on his chest, two faces of Janus rooted, looking to the future and to the past; the god of transitions. He was exactly this for me. I worshiped, paid alms to the altar I was splayed across all night. My god, the way that man made love to me. I clawed into his back. Sucked the inked head of his Janus tattoo on his shoulder. He turned me and slapped me and fucked like the god painted on him. Then turned me over and fucked me like the twin that looked back. I can not believe I don't have an std. This is the real miracle.

The next morning, he left early and came back with croissants and orange juice and wrote me a letter in french that I could not read. I took the train back to Paris and cried until I pulled my suitcase onto the platform, wiped my eyes with the back of my hand and yelled out loud right there on the platform.

"Fuuuuuuck!!!!!!" I had reached my end of numb. I didn't want to keep him. I didn't even want to keep the man from Lyon that was maybe dead. I wanted to keep the me I was with them. I wanted to keep the woman that didn't exist beyond what I had told him. He didn't know I had children and that I had to go home and walk into a fire and officially divorce my husband of ten years who was being heartless to me now that he had a girlfriend. He didn't know I had to figure out a way to pay my rent. He didn't know me at all.

I wanted to keep the woman that asked for happy birthday full body worship and got it an hour later.

I wanted to keep my black velvet cat with her ass in the air. Outside of motherhood. Outside of the United States courts and the system that profited from me weak. Outside of old drunk rich dudes that snored. Outside of dependence and rent due and threats to my motherhood. Outside of liars and porsches and Los Angeles bullshit. Outside of reality.

I didn't want to keep him.
I wanted to keep the woman in the story I told him.

I didn't want to keep him.

I wanted to keep me.

That was the first time I knew that.
And that was good to know.

i came to paris the reason we all do
but i came to lyon because
i still love you.
and i loved you most
the night you had the map on your lap
and pointed.
i will not tell you i came.
there was only one rose left
in the parc de la tete d'or
i did not reach.
i took nothing from you.
every stone i picked up i put back.
wherever you are you can stay.
i've tried forgetting you
they're right it's worse that way
so i thought i'd try the train.
that's fucked you would say.
but you are the one that
taught me the song and
it will not stop playing
so
you can not
blame
me
for
singing

DOCTOR

When I was dating the pathological liar, and spending nights in his Orange County mansion, I woke suddenly and jumped out of bed. This time, I didn't wake because his drunk on cognac unconscious body ripped the comforter off me, and I didn't wake because of the earthquake that I was sure was going to cause the waves that would hit the bedroom window to tsunami us. No, I woke because the most beautiful man in the whole wide world that I had never seen came to my dream and knocked on the inside of my ribcage. And though I had never seen this most beautiful man in the whole wide world, what I didn't know then was that I would very soon.

In the dream, while I was laying beside the pathological liar in his house with the waves beating against the window, this gorgeous man with brown skin and black curly hair and black eyes came up behind me with a thick spanish accent and said, "He's lying to you. You're right about everything, Dian." Then deep in my subconscious, he took me to a window and showed me all the faces of the women he was lying about and said to leave right now and never look back–that he was coming soon.

Being the delusional woman I am–with no evidence of his cheating or the reality of the dream man or the women's faces–I, at three thirty-three a.m., grabbed my clothes hanging in the closet, my makeup bag from his master bathroom, my shoes, shut the front door like a whisper, got into my cold Jeep and raced down the Pacific Coast Highway through marine layer home.

The drunk pathological liar man snoring in his Orange County mansion on the ocean didn't notice that I left until eleven a.m. the next day, when his old man body peed and ripped off his nose snore strip and rubbed the circles under his eyes. He was tall and hot and booming and terrifying with a great cock. He was waking up from heavy swigs of cognac that I heard him drink throughout the night (that he refused to admit he slammed). See, he was "sober". After I swore to him I would leave if he drank again, that I wouldn't tolerate his rages, he said it was easy for him to stop since he wasn't an alcoholic, then hid a green glass bottle of Remy Martin under his side of the bed to swig in the middle of the night. At one point, even though I went to medical school, I was actually googling, *does it for sure mean you're an alcoholic if you wake up to drink in the middle of the night?*

Google answered right away.
Yes. Yes. Turns out it does.

When I caught him, he would say that is how he was so good in bed and so I had to choose great sex or for him to stop drinking. We did have great sex. Mainly because he was Satan himself and fucked like he was about to burn me for eternity. I loved his penis. It was better than average but he kept begging to stick it in my ass which made it slightly less than average.

He wore a shirt to michelin restaurants that said -*ASSHOLE*- that he justified by saying everyone was a narcissist! Not just him! Anyway, he was clearly better than everyone and I knew it, he said, because at least he admitted it! Everyone else was a fucking coward! Name one man that was brave and hot as him! He said this made him more cowboy than any cowboy and more rockstar than any rockstar.

I was just happy that when I opened his palms there was always a fire there.

I hated him. I loved him. I hated him. He would cry during sex and I would hold this six foot five man that would tell me I was the best sex of his life and if I ever left him he would kill me and the man I thought I loved after him. Though he assured me that was impossible because I would never love anyone but him again. How could I? I was fucking a god, everyone else was mortals.

He hid everything, the texts, the bills, the second phone, the nonexistent certifications, the cognac bottles, one underneath his bathroom sink, one in his tv cabinet, under his bed, in the corner of his garage. The drunk man in the orange county mansion taking swigs of cognac with his espresso that I was not allowing in my ass called himself a Doctor. All of his letters were addressed 'Doctor—'. He told me once he lived for ten years for free by collecting student aid and traveling around Europe to write poetry that he swore the world was not worthy of and was infinitely better than my own. He maxed out every credit card then found a loophole to get them to write it all off. Later, I would find out that the loophole was his name change. He had four names. One of these men lived in Boulder, one in Miami, one in San Francisco, and the one that I knew, though didn't know at all, lived in Orange County.

One time, we were sitting at a bar and he got drunk and mean and he told the bartender he was a much better writer than me and I stormed out of the restaurant. He chased me out without paying and pulled his Maserati behind me in the parking lot trapping me. When I jumped the curb and got on the PCH, he raced in front of me and slammed on his brakes, and kept swerving toward the side of my car. I was terrified and screaming prayers. A cop sitting at the gas station saw him and pulled him over. I was certain he would be arrested and given a DWI. I raced home ahead of the sirens and locked all of my doors and laid in my bed frozen. He texted me twenty minutes later. *I explained to him and he understood.*

To this day I wonder how much he paid him.

It took a one month BeenVerified membership to find out he was a 'naturopath healer' that went to some two year hippie Colorado school. He did a "residency" in acupuncture in Thailand. God, I should have known then. I suspected the truth one day when we were laying in bed the morning after our third date. I said, "Percuss my lung doctor!" He flicked me. I said, "You don't remember?"

"Of course not!" he said. "That's for family medicine doctors. Not for real doctors, psychiatrists like me. That is way below me!"

"Where did you go to school, Doctor?" I asked.

"The best school in the world" he said.

"Oh I see Doctor. Where is the best school in the world?"

"This is below me," he said, taking a swig of fernet, that he referred to as 'grounding medicine'.

"Ok Doctor," I said.

Even if he wasn't lying, *which he was*, how did this man who claimed to be a doctor, seeing five patients a week over the phone, afford a twenty million dollar mansion on the ocean? I didn't care if he had money. I just wanted to crack the code. He kept me curious and I loved it. He kept me feeling pissed, kept me burning and I loved it. Because I wasn't supposed to love it, I loved it. Sure, doctors are rich in the midwest but they aren't rich in Orange County. Doctors don't have Maseratis and three hundred and fifty thousand dollar Bentleys and own twenty million dollar beach mansions. He said he had "investments".

But it was hot, too, the mystery dressed in his outrageous designer black leather. One time, he wore a priest costume to dinner, freeballing, his cock free and hard underneath. You could see the outline of it through the priest dress. Fucking weirdo. I loved how everyone looked at us, how we snuck into every restaurant without reservations and sat where we wanted to sit and no one dared ask us anything. I loved how people stared, how we were bigger than life, how he celebrated my outrage. I loved putting acupuncture needles into his back and legs and ass, putting red lipstick on him, how I straddled him at restaurants and he'd grab my ass with both of his big hands putting on a show for the world. He was in the wild wild west. When the waiter asked us to leave, he said, "I'm almost cumming. Then we'll be done."

"Let's get out of here," I said.

"She needs cock. We have to go right now." He announced to the entire restaurant in a priest robe.

Listen, I am Calamity Jane. He was the kind of man that would shoot the sheriff. He was the kind of man that would break me out of a foreign prison. He was the kind of man that would fight a child for a yoyo. Every single night, the man would lay on top of me, holding me down, telling me how hot it was that I was submitting to him. That if I just let him just once put it in my ass he would bring me to another dimension. "You know why I want to put it in your ass?" he asked, one time drunker than hell. "Because I'm putting you in a place of humiliation. Showing you who is boss, little girl."

I was sickly proud of myself and my acting skills, how hard it made him. When he tied me up my double joints could easily escape, so I'd act as if I was unable to move. I pressed my wrists into the ropes I could break free from and then pretended to be tied down while he fucked me.

How many of us women are pressing our wrists into loose ropes pretending to be tied down?

Laying on me he told me that there was nowhere I could go. But I knew I could push him off, cut off his balls with my teeth. It was a game I played. Allowing a man I deeply hated to force me to submit. Knowing he could never actually accomplish this turned me on. Before him, I had no idea the darkness, the hate for my own soul that allowed this even existed. It was good to know, to look it in the eye so that I could purge it from my cells like black soot after frog poison in the jungle. But first, I needed to observe it through the cage, ensure it was breathing, like watching a monster at the end of a rifle. No need to shoot and awaken the world unless you know your enemy is still alive.

He refused to carry anything heavy for me. I was the farmgirl, he said. I had worker blood. He was from high class. But then, in the next breath he would say that I was a god like him and therefore better than everyone. That was the only reason he wanted to impregnate me you see, because he wanted to make a god and it took two gods to make a god. He said often that he was going to marry me and that his fantasy was when he came in me during our wedding night, that I would get pregnant with his son and we would name him Zeus. I laughed so hard I cried. That pissed him off.

He once fought a comedian. We went to a comedy show and sat on the front row and the comedian made a joke about me being young and hot with an old guy and he stomped his big black boots on the stage and boomed, "Shut the fuck up you ugly fucktard!"

He wouldn't stop screaming at the guy the rest of the set. He ruined the entire night for everyone. His sole and soul purpose was to ruin the world for everyone. Also, I am certain he had autism. Hot. He'd tell people his public outbursts were to defend me but it was always an ego- reaction, his narcissism and insecurities lit on fire. I finally said, "Baby, let's leave." He stormed out and threatened the popcorn man at the small theater entrance. Soon after, a man chased him outside. I saw a gun at his belt.

"Get in the car! Get in the fucking car now!" I screamed.

On the way home, he said he felt like a King and that I was his Queen in the mead hall. Front row. While the army watched and cheered. He said he loved how I was unafraid and stoic, how he had never before had a woman that was not embarrassed of him.

"Why is everyone such fucking pussies? I just want to play with the world! No one will play with me! All these LA snowflakes! I'm going to send them to the war to die." He yelled about the state of the world all the way home. What I knew was if he didn't yell he would cry.

I have never fucked anyone like I fucked him that night. There were things I loved. I loved his wild. I loved his unapologetic force. His bravery. His ego.
And I hated it all in equal measure.

I had to keep reminding myself I was with a scam artist. I made him watch the movie, Catch Me If You Can. He loved it. "Wow. I really relate," he said. "Let's watch it again."

If I ever show up dead, ask my best friend. She knows his name and hates him and will lead authorities straight to his front door- and guess what? That's not even his front door.

He had to nightly answer calls from his "assistant" that came in the middle of dinner, in the middle of a movie, in the middle of making love.

"It's just this woman I pay to get my mail in New York," he said. "Why are you so jealous? Can I not have an assistant?!"

I stayed as long as I had to find the truth. I tested him often, the witch in me subconsciously strapping him to a boiling pot of stew to interrogate. I was losing my mind. I couldn't confirm anything. One time, I parked outside his house begging God for answers. When he heard me laying on my horn he sat in my passenger seat and denied everything. When he stood to go inside, his phone fell out of his deep leather shorts pocket and onto the passenger seat and he slammed the door. Thank you angels. I drove off with it. I knew the code. Old men are idiots about their passwords. It was his birthday backwards.

I read hundreds of texts from his women "patients". He was telling them they were magical, not crazy, and they were sending paragraphs of their psychoses and their fantasies of him. He didn't send his fantasies back but he encouraged theirs. They shared songs and movie recommendations together and he asked in great detail about it all saying it was important for his evaluation. He championed their intuitive powers in the higher realms. He said they were psychic and magical not crazy! They were misunderstood by the medical system.

These women were madly in love.

His healing powers were only for women. Just like you Chelsie. He said.

I hated that and I loved that about him. He believed no one was crazy. We had this in common. Though I think maybe this is easy to do when you are the craziest of all.

"It's important they fall in love with me," he would tell me.

"This is the opposite of my work," I told him. "You're using vulnerable women."

"I'm healing them!"

He explained how he helped them incorporate back into society without being locked up or on medication. There was truth to this too, but the man wasn't a psychiatrist. However he was extremely educated. Brilliant. Maybe more than any psychiatrist I had ever met in medical school.

I was so conflicted I lost fifteen pounds in three months. I got two root canals. My body was fighting itself.

When I would question anything, he'd scream, towering over me and spit in my face while describing in detail everything about me that was below him.

His "assistant" turned out to be a rich woman he met at a conference. They had an affair as he manipulated her "healing her from her psychosis" and broke up their marriages. She had millions, they invested in things together. Those things did very well. It was her money. All of it. Everything he had was a gift from this woman for healing her.

In the car that day I read his texts to this woman- telling her she couldn't come this weekend because he was busy. He texted her about selling her house, the house he claimed was his third home when he brought me there the weekend of my birthday. He put all of her things in large plastic tupperware tubs in the garage. While he was sleeping one morning I opened them. Each of them full of women's clothes my size.

Why were the house cameras turned off that weekend? she wanted to know in the texts.

Because I was fucking my new girlfriend in your house, he didn't say. Instead, he replied, *They must have had a power shortage.*

I was watching the door and if he caught me looking at his phone, I would say I was changing the song on the speaker system. I had seen his temper flare. I didn't know what would happen to me if I told him I knew he was lying.

One time, in my questioning, he called me a stupid bitch and I took the cognac glass out of his hand and shattered it at his feet. He grabbed my wrists until I bruised, holding me down on his couch. When I got free, I ran and grabbed the painting off his wall that one of the women he fucked had painted. The sliding glass door was open to the ocean crashing. I ran with it above my head to throw it in the black water.

I don't remember the next thirty minutes of wrestling with him but I left with bruises.

The sex and violence was just a cover for the lies. It was maddening and something in me loved unraveling it. I didn't know then if I was staying because I needed to know what it was like to fuck Satan or because every mitochondria in me was burning for the truth of this liar. I know why now.
It was because he always kept me entertained. Everyone else bored the hell out of me.
Have you ever fucked until you cried, had him wipe your crying wet face, not pausing and keep fucking? Well it's great, ok, and I highly recommend it. So there's that too.

I thought I loved him. The truth is I did love what he did to the depths of me, lost in a storm at sea. I loved that I was in a boat I knew would never come home. I loved that we were out of the matrix. I love that Wild Bill Hickock was mine and hated by the world and may be shot in the back at any moment.

I had learned to sleep through the roar, that beach house felt like being on a boat that was lost in a storm. Something in me loved that I could sleep in a house like that. Him pulling the covers off me nightly, sleeping with a pillow over his balding head. Satan doesn't need to breathe.

Just like the woman, Katie, was not his assistant, the intern woman that lived at his gallery, and the woman who came to his house to cut his hair, who glared at me at his gallery nights, weren't who he said they were either.

Christmas eve, I looked over his shoulder when he was texting her and reached for his phone. He choked me on his bed until I lost consciousness. When I came to, he threw me around the room by my hair like a rag doll with my children downstairs, unaware. When I finally got free, and ran downstairs, he screamed at my kids, "YOUR MOTHER IS A STUPID WHORE!"

I said, "He's being silly and drunk. Run to the car."

They still don't know what happened. I took them to CVS and let them pick out $500 that I didn't have worth of Christmas toys. When I got back in the Jeep, there were bruises the perfect size of his fingers over my neck, still red, though I watched them turn brown a few hours after the kids went to sleep and the blood settled. I kept running my hands over my neck, remembering bruises are broken vessels where the blood pools. He broke my vessels and made my blood pool outside of them. While the marks settled into dark fingertips, I woke up sore and numb and zombied through, hosting a perfect Christmas morning for my children wearing a turtleneck.

When they went to their dad's house the next day, I boarded a flight to Paris. I would teach Jeanne D'Arc from the place that burnt her alive. Rouen. He wrote me a hundred emails that weren't apologies but excuses that I received in the middle of the night while he was drunk on cognac. Most of them were incoherent ramblings of a man who decided to do bufo and was experiencing latent hallucinations. They were full of insults that my poetry was terrible or I was ugly or stupid or I would never amount to anything. That his work was more important. That he made more money. That I am scared of real love. That this was all my fault. That I am a jealous bitch. That he was Jesus Christ come again and came to this planet as an alien and he was going to take me from earth to his planet when I died.

I tried to block his email, but he made new email addresses. Daily.

I thought you liked me to choke you in bed, one read.

I didn't respond. When I flew home I promised to meet with him to get my things. It was important for me to look him in the eye. I had to get myself out of his home. There were so many of my favorites things that I missed at his place, many of which were sentimental. I would not let him take more from me. I made up my mind. I had to be brave and face him again.

The first time I was back in his house, I told my best friend to call the cops if I hadn't texted her in an hour. I walked upstairs. He followed me closely. On the way to the closet, I opened the guest room door, and found the first of two altars to me. He quickly shut it. "Let me see. I think it's so sexy you did this," I lied. I walked over, taking a video from my phone in my pocket he didn't realize I took. "That's my scarf? My underwear? My lip gloss? My book? But I didn't leave any of this here! You are... wild." My voice was shaking, it took everything in me to hide my fear. I smiled at him and picked it all off his altar. There was melted candle wax on the crotch of my panties burnt through and what I am certain was his ejaculate crusted over them. A chill went down my spine.

He had climbed up the canyon and broke in through a back window while I was in Rouen and stole everything special to me, my silk floral scarf, my red undies and ripped pages and pages out of my diaries. Every love poem I had written about a past ex was gone. He was erasing my poetry. There was no greater sin. I wanted him dead. I was too afraid to report him. I knew what he was capable of.

"Get a gun," my father told me.

He asked me to sit down on his bed and talk with him.

"Show me what you have in the bag in your closet and I'll sit down with you."

When I tore open the trash bag, ninety percent of my things I left were there. I told him I was going to put it in the car. He grabbed my grandmother's silk scarf out of my hand so I would have to come back inside. While I was sitting with him, he handed me his phone to show a painting he was working on. I panned out quickly to his photos. He had taken photos of my entire house. One of them was of my passport, meaning I was home–maybe at the grocery store or picking up my children from school while he was breaking into my house.

"Why do you have a picture of my passport? Did you hire a PI? Am I being followed? Tell me the truth!" I said, suddenly remembering he had hired a PI to follow his ex wife. He ripped the phone out of my hands.

"I did," he said.

"And what did you find out? What the fuck did you find on me?"

"I got your divorce records," he said. "Turns out you are divorced and you really do make your own money."

"No shit, you psycho!"

I was shaking. I felt it. I knew for months I was being watched. Followed. I thought I was being paranoid at the time but I could feel it. I was right. He admitted everything. He broke into my home for months every time I was out of the country teaching, which was every other week. My intuition was confirmed every time I came back. He knew where to go to miss the ring cameras, my son's room. The camera only caught him once. He parked down the hill and climbed up the canyon through the cactus and broke into the old window that had no lock. He pushed out the screen. I could feel his energy in my house as soon as I got home. How did I know? I am a woman. I knew. Then he started showing up where I was in town. I was sure after the third time that he had put a tracker on my jeep.

For four months after this conversation, he sent multiple insane narcissistic emails daily, roses dipped in gold to my house, and even sewed king sized sheets together to make a banner on his house 'CHELSIE COME HOME' written in dark red. Probably pig blood from the spell of an old witch.

I started looking for houses frantically in gated neighborhoods because I knew I could no longer stay where I was with the hope of remaining alive. I could no longer sleep. I put the kids in my room on mattresses. I called the cops and reported everything so they would have records. "There is nothing we can do ma'am," was all they said over and over.

I had to make more money so I could afford safety. I looked at gated communities that would cost me three times my rent. I had to work my ass off. I prayed hard, the women kept coming to class. I had enough students to take the leap.

Women, once again, would save me.

The day I moved in, I installed twenty-three cameras inside and around my house, and I felt like a god.

I made a spectacle of it. Knowing he was stalking my instagram, I put the installation videos all over my stories and told the world that I was collecting evidence against my ex who was breaking into my home.

After that, I never heard from him again, except for one email. He wrote that he had spent a hundred thousand dollars on the top psychic healers in the world, and that he was Archangel Michael and came back to the earth to save it and that if I didn't return to him this life, he would find me in the next. *They are the top level spiritual masters, very secret I can not tell you my sources. You are not high enough to access them*, he wrote. In the next sentence, he said that we were working out karma, that I was a little servant girl in every past life he saved from an evil king that locked me up and raped me.

I wrote back before I blocked him. *Interesting, I talked to the best psychic in the world too and she told me I was actually the King and that you were my little bitch in every life which is why you love the ass."*

I know he laughed out loud when he read that and I know he typed up a long email about how I was low level karma and would never amount to anything without him that I would never read because I blocked him immediately.

I also know that after he spent hours sending the cruelest email you can imagine, the asshole that I will always love, bent his knees to face the setting sun and my stolen pair of underwear
and prayed for me to come home.

when my man talks about any woman
who happens to be remotely in love with him
who paints a painting for his wall
or sends him a scholarly article on the pulitzer
i become very unenlightened
and decide it's time for me to burn my cardiac valves
in the white flame of dante's inferno.
oh fuck off!
i know it's not ok to want a human all to yourself
this is a world with lots of humans you say!
and the screenwriters in venice
will tell you monogamy is for the birds!
the cormorants in fact!
(which i certainly was in a very recent life)
my shaman will tell you
he has to talk to pretty girls, ugly girls
to exist in the world
and i tell her the ugly ones are the worst!
we have to make up for our stance against botox
with great poetry
and annie hall neckties
and stories of cinque terre!
you should feel the relief i feel
when i realize the friend
he is telling the quite lovely story about is a man
i would rather be alone than want to possess another human
in the way i absolutely positively must possess my human!
so what if i want him all to myself?
so what if i slept with my head in his armpit
to smell my hair all day
so what that she has as much sexual energy
as a goldman sachs employee
a grey stone on the beach of his life
so what that still i took that stone
and rubbed it against my own bone
and it lit a fire i swallowed
and then walked up stairs to bed
with the cup of hot tea

and breathed flames
no smaller
than the size
of my terrible
love for him.

you've pulled me out
spitting salt not ready to die

i'm the patient that wakes up swinging

the scorpion at the bottom of the pool
holding her breath for six days
tail up!

i sit at the bar and make you jealous
i sit at the bar and talk about kissing girls
i sit at the bar and tell you
i don't care about your stupid fashion
and take off your coat

i outta straighten you out like a piece of wire

i outta call an uber to drive me hundred miles home!

i outta be madder than hell.

you told the man at the comedy club
'you don't look at her fuckhole'
you told the man at the comedy club
you were going to put a bullet in his head!

some women just want a man
who is nice to them.
those kids had granite counter tops!
those kids got everything they asked for for christmas!

i already drowned the painter of oceans.

i want you caravaggio.
attending public beheadings
for the accurate angle of the spurt

i want you
that knows if you walk the same pace as the rain

you get less wet

i want you
because you know how to hold onto a ledge

there is a horrible inexhaustible truth.
buttoned in a dress too small

that we do not choose who we love

this is what the birds keep singing.

your therapist doesn't know shit
she's a bored god sitting on some mountain
jealous of our mortality

you better know our blood is always fighting.
you better know those leukocytes have fists!
peace? ha! when chaos is our circle!
when the smallest of us is warring to stay here?

it's always been
that masked thing
when someone you love
dies in the night
and you suddenly wake.

it's always been the eyes
of a some big cat
you know is
stalking you on the trail

or that thing
at the end of the world
when there is a taste of fear.

some say they broke up a meteor last week
because they know what's coming for us.

but this is the day before that

this is the day
i sit on your counter
and i don't say it
but
i love you
more than i have ever
loved you before

i've climbed under barbed wire and hooked my back on you.
if you don't stop looking at me like you
have never loved like this i will
juliet the knife and split my liver open!
i will jump into a sepia photograph!
into one of our hard knock lives!
one without air-conditioning and pasteurization
where you have to drive a donkey plow
you're such a pain in the ass
i walk twenty steps ahead of you
in the malibu country mart
i leave the canyon pizza place
i call bullshit! at fred segal
and the stupid security man
guarding $70 mushroom shorts
who has never
ever caught anyone shoplifting
in this town ever
asks if we're ok?
no i'm not ok.
jesus cast my demons into the swine
i tell you i like fighting with you.
you tell me i'm sadistic.
you tell me i'm too soft to live in new york.
i tell you god loves me best
you tell me prove it
i tell you she gave me your perfect cock
my favorite cock in the whole wide brutal beautiful world
full of perfectly fine but lesser beautiful cocks

my ex husband one terrible day at the end
a new moon past our funeral
my ex husband said like a old owl
that you walk deep into the forest to consult
with a handful of shiny offerings
tinsel, and chips of stained glass,
and broken iridescent shells
(all i had left from the explosion)
he took in his beak

and said
"he will have brown eyes"
"he will be creative"
"he will be fire."
you in the chemical of me
so deep even he could taste you.

so listen up. you were wrong.
you're not going to fuck weak girls
that wash your feet in oil
that you can never love
until you die.
you're not going to drink the demons
or look too hard at the knives.
you're not going to let the orchard die
or keep the dead roses.
you're sure as hell are not going to walk into the sea
and never return.
no.
you're going to walk in a kitchen that's singing in my voice
that smells like breakfast.
because despite you saying
a thousand times
woman!
how many times do i have to tell you?
i can't eat nine eggs!

i once again
have
made you
nine eggs.

The man was not just in my dream. He exists.

you exist
your burned boots
stomping out the neighbor's fire
on your horse named ramona.
you exist the atlantean's hymn
you exist what survived the flood.
you exist brown. sipping mezcal
and singing me a language
which i can not sing yet
but i swear to you
i will sing
yet
you exist.
and i am a circus clown in the parking lot
handing out fliers
come see the greatest show on earth!
you exist.
come to my house and tackle me
tie my arms above my head
call the calvary!
press me in medieval torture device
nail beds from two sides
sink them in my pancreas
siphon my sugar.
bottle my insulin for the world
oh i have touched the torture wheel
it will fall apart!
so bless me a saint!
paint my head on a 16th century platter!
paint me a new name for blue!
paint me a melting glacier
still sharp below the atlantic
don't you dare come between us
i will numb you
and sharp you
and puncture pull
deep you
s i n k
i will sink you

treacherous
flying on one wing you
and then i will name your leg freckles
your arm freckles
learn every star under
your burning sky
you exist and i will make into beasts
all the men in the shrub
peering at diana
you exist
i point all my spikes and shrapnel
and cuboid finger bones
to you
oh i'm in trouble-
the mob boss is crying.
he has strung me up
like pheasant in granddaddies basement
the blood is to my head.
pluck me pluck me
pluuuuuuck me
mi amor
i will eat your fingers like carrots and
regrow a lizard tail
i will start a war

with the disease
of my pull
you exist
i am 17.
frida kahlo hiding in the auditorium
watching diego
watching you
paint a woman
watching you paint a woman
that looks exactly like me.
you exist
and i stand on the moth stage
tap the microphone
a single light on me
to tell all who will listen

tell all who will listen
a story
about
your
hands.

HIM

There is a story that happened to me, more than anything that has happened to me, and even now, though it is more mine than anything has ever been mine, not even I feel qualified to tell it. It's like talking about the robbery when you still have the gun to your head. It's like I am reaching my hand through the cage of an animal that has a mouth big enough to swallow me whole. I know there are teeth in this that could kill me. Or worse, not kill, just shred, leave me staring at the last inch of my life for the rest of my life. For the past few years, I have been running furiously away from this place, the place he touched in me.

I am a world record breaker. Not the fastest, but damn my endurance. I will run to guard the open wound my whole life long. There is no catching me for salve or suture. There is no end to how far I will go. And by now I know I will never stop.

I moved to Mexico because I fell deeper in love than I have ever been. I still don't know what happened except that he was the man that came to me in the dream telling me to leave. He, the most beautiful man I had never seen, said he was coming for me.

And he came for me.

Months after the dream I was in Coyoacan teaching Frida Kahlo from her home.

The night before class, Frida came to me in a fevered dream except I had no fever. Lucid, I think they call it. She wanted me to listen. She told me who to teach and I wrote down the list. She put cracks in my spine and promised the pain would leave when she left–that I was just feeling her pain. She told me if I did what she said, she would give me something. I was afraid then of what I am sure of now, that she had awakened Diego from his painted coffin and brought him by his paint stained hands straight to me.

It's exactly what she did.

He was making a movie about her. The first thing he sent was a video from his home in Mexico. He was standing through the interior courtyard of his home, zooming through layers of glass walls to the living room, past the black baby grand, to the shelf, to the book cover, then to Frida Kahlo's eye. Frida's eye, inside his glass house, the house that I, in just a few months, would be fully unpacked and living in, dreaming in, next to him in, repeating in Spanish the word forever in. Para siempre.

I sent him a video of the same book by candlelight on my table. Same Frida's eye.

Is that you? I asked.

Where?

In the reflection. The only way we'd ever be seen.

I remember you, I wrote.

I remember you, he wrote.

I had come to him before in dreams, too, with wings, walking toward the ocean.

And where were you in your dream? I wrote back.

He was standing behind me, watching me. Unmoving.

He was standing behind me, watching me. Unmoving.

I knew then. Though I had hoped with the hope that keeps prisoners living in concrete cells without light their whole lives, I knew then I was using my own blood to tally my days on the wall.

What he did was much worse than Lucifer before him. He touched an early part of me that had never been awake, a part unreachable by my children or friends or work or even poetry. He tapped at it incessantly, as if to wake a patient under anesthetic. The patient woke and would never sleep again. The patient was starving. The patient was fed enough to live forever, to run and not stop, to make sure our love would not die before it did. Then he crushed the drug and I drank it bitter. Glasses and glasses of serotonin rushing to drain the chemical of me, filled me filled me filled me, made love to me like a god, like a king, like love makes love to love, and then sent me emptied of myself on a plane home. I was ordered to return to my dreams, to the land of night, the land of Frida. The only way I would ever be able to keep him was if I could cut off everything that had nerves and stay sleeping. I repeated over and over. I don't ache when he leaves. *I don't ache when he leaves.*

The only voice that answered promised, *if you want to leave him to see your children you have to numb. If you want to keep him you have to numb. You have to bury your fire, your desires alive.*

Who was I kidding? I have never been able to do that.

I begged him to be sharper, a knifepoint breaking into my house and stealing my underwear for his altar. I wanted him tearing out my journal pages and ruining my silk scarves. I wanted him putting trackers on my Jeep and bruising my neck. I wanted him to want me illegally. Dangerously. Unapologetically. I didn't care how, I just wanted him wanting me like I wanted him.

The night I had unpacked thirteen suitcases in Mexico City, I bought matching closet hangers and a toothbrush holder at the mall. "I love seeing you here. Your clothes by my clothes, your toothbrush, your hair in the drain." he said making while love to me.

We walked home from dinner, lost in a monstrous love that drowned us below her tongue. I wandered into an old bookstore and bought him a poetry book and he bought handcarved wooden birds for my children that he would never meet.

We painted that night. I read him my novel. When I looked up he was wiping his eyes. His feet in my lap. I have never had a man love my words like he loved my words. He felt the poetry of me.

"You're my favorite writer in the world Dian. Wow...wow," he repeated. "Wow."

He built a home in Valle de Bravo and we went there every weekend. He was a cowboy, my cowboy, his boots, his hands, his horses, how he cut downed trees for firewood, a round pen, a stable. He had a team of local Mexican men that worked for him. One day, I walked into his office in Mexico City and he was handing the head of construction a briefcase full of cash. I sat in the corner and tried to use the 'translate' feature on my phone. He was yelling. The man didn't get the suitcase. He was sorry.

When he left, I asked, "You were angry?"

"Yes," he answered. "If you do the job right, I am happy. Do the job wrong, I am not. Thin ice? That's the english? Thin ice."

I loved how men were terrified of him. But I hated how no one gave me a second look. It was my own fault, I was playing a part. I would stand in the shower every night and know it, too. Everyone thought I was his little white girl side piece and yet my business was booming, at an all time high. He was making good money, but I did the math and I was sure I was making as much or more than him. He had an army of men and respect and maids and nannies and drivers and cooks and secretaries and dozens of employees and businesses. All I had to show for my success was an entire life that revolved around him. I was not only his equal, in the eyes of capitalism, I was his superior. I would never ever acknowledge this fact, and it would never ever be acknowledged. I had forsaken everything for us. But I was a poet, and wasn't that the point?

Had I ever once in my life stood in front of a human I loved and been equally seen, acknowledged in my full power, honored for it? I was trying to convince myself it was romantic to give myself to someone. To bleed on the cross for the love that put me there.

The land in Valle de Bravo was where I wanted to spend the rest of my life. Because the land was his body. His body was my home. I put on two of his coats and slept outside with him under the stars. The thing is there are more stars when you are living in the dark. I straddled him and sang him country songs he didn't know and kissed his eyelids, his perfect cheekbones. *Te amo. Y Aqui. Te amo. Y Aqui. Aqui. Aqui.*

How do you say you are mine?
How do you say my soul started with your soul?
How do you say same star?
How do you say your skin makes me cry?

The neighbor's mutts and the stray german shepherd slept outside with us to protect us. When a man would walk down the jungle trail in the middle of the night, the german shepherd would take off after him. We would have to stop her from ripping out the stranger's throat.

"I want to adopt her," I told him. "Can she be mine?"

"She is yours," he said. "You can have whatever you want Dian. Whatever you want."

"I want you. Promise me I can have you."

"Why do you do this? You have me. You have me."

"Her name is Mildred. Millie for short."

He laughed.

"Mildred. Me calling this guard dog around all my men. Mildred!"

"Yes. Esta Bien. I want your men with guns yelling Mildred!"

"You are crazy, Dian. Crazy."

"How did you find this place? It's magic."

"Dian, you see the armored trucks in town? This is cartel land. You have to know family. You have to be *in*. I have friends that let me in."

He looked at me and raised his eyebrows. We never had to speak the same language because we spoke the same language. He was my nerve ending, my fingertips, everything I loved under one flesh, my whole world. If he said he was the head of the cartel, the truth is I would have helped him bury bodies. I would have carried a machine gun, dyed and sawed off my hair in a kitchen sink and swore my entire identity away to be his.

"I don't care. I love you. Whatever it is. You can tell me.."

"Amor, it's Mexico. It's no secret. There are good guys and bad guys. You mind your business and the bad guys don't bother you. You are fine. You have to be smart."

I wondered who were the bad guys? Who were the good guys?

"Tell me you love me."

"I love you so fucking much." He gritted his teeth and grabbed my face and kissed me hard.

One day, when we were outside by the stables, a group of a hundred men rushed through the gate on horseback with guns onto his property through to the neighbor's property behind. "Go inside," he told me, and saddled up and rode behind them. I did what he said. I always did what he said. There was yelling. Dogs fought. A gunshot or two. Then the men rode back through the field and left. One of them saw me in the window. I remember looking at him through my reflection. I was wearing a plaid shirt with two braids. I nodded my head. I should hide. Why was I unafraid? I know why. I had a love I would've happily died for. And if anything, that's what makes us unafraid. He talked outside with one of his men that I recognized from his construction projects. An hour or so later he came in.

"This is Gabrielo's land. That man stopped paying rent. It was time for him to leave the property."

"Did he leave?" I asked.

"Oh yes, he left."

"Why do they have access through your property to theirs?"

"Do you not understand? They have access wherever they want. I wouldn't be here if they didn't sell me this land. We're friends."

Every Saturday, we went riding through the jungle mountains on his horses. The first time we left to ride I was surprised we would not be going alone. When we were saddled up suddenly a man showed up outside the house on a horse, a handgun strapped to his belt and a big leather bag.

"He is Pedro. He protect you."

From who? I didn't ask.

"Pedro. Dian."

When we started riding, he rode up beside me on the trail.

"Dian. Do not get off trail. Pedro will ride in front and I behind. If they stop us, do not say a word in english. You look Mexicana. Skin brown. Es good. Be quiet. I know that's hard for you." He smiled in his hat. His dark curls underneath. I smiled back. I wasn't afraid, I was turned on. I was in awe. I was madly, incandescently in love. I wasn't in my life anyway. If I died in this one, wouldn't I wake up in the other–in California with my babies where I spoke the language?

"Stay alive. Todos bien. Perfect day to be with my woman and my horse in my Mexico," he said.

"Te amo."

"Te amo," he silently mouthed, pulling back so I would ride up in front of him.

An hour in, he whipped his horse and took off through a river and a field after my german shepherd. She was about to kill a lamb in a field before us. I have never seen a man ride a horse like that, "YA!!!! YA!!!!!" past me like a blur, his spurs sunk into her side.

He stopped Millie before she sunk her teeth in, riding between the dog and lamb. Then he jumped off his horse while it was still moving and grabbed the german shepherd by the skin of her neck lifting her off the ground.

Pedro yelled something in Spanish and took her from him, keeping an eye on her. She yipped. She understood. He took a rope from his bag and tied her to his horse.

We sat by the cold river, our feet in the water. Pedro with the gun stayed on the horse to patrol the dogs while we ate what his maid packed us for lunch.

"You kill their sheep, they don't come for your dog. They come for you. If she would have got the sheep. Pedro knows to shoot the dog."

Every muscle in my body was tight. I thought about how every time we fought, I came for his sheep. How I was on a rope. How there was never a negotiation. No working on things. He loved me. He loved that dog. But he'll shoot the dog.

That night, I gave him his birthday present. A spanish edition of The Count of Monte Cristo, our favorite novel as children that we both read in different languages, in different countries. I lit candles in a circle around a picnic blanket. He said he was going to build the kids a treehouse where we were dancing. We danced to Harvest Moon playing on my phone over and over and over and over. The fourth time Neil Young sang, I said,

"When we get married, lets do it right here, in Valle, on our land, in this place under the stars."

"I will have as many babies as you want," I told him. "I will write my books. And we will write our movies and we will travel, less when the baby comes, but we will travel whenever you want and you will build our home here. Wabi Sabi like you like. The library. The bookcase under the big glass windows. The bathtub with the board you cut yourself. I want your mama to move in with us soon so I can take care of her and love her like my own."

His eyes were wet.

"And I will forever ride on the back of your motorcycle and push off of semis."

He laughed, wiping his eyes with the back of his hand. Earlier that week, he had taken me on a five hour motorcycle ride to the middle of Mexico to a cafeteria just so I could taste his childhood, the most authentic delicious food I have and will ever taste. On the way on the laneless highway a semi truck bumped into us and I put out my arm and pushed our bike away from it and we almost crashed.

"I don't care if a semi brushes you on the highway, you never push it away! You could have killed us both," he said.

I knew he was probably right, but what I didn't know was this was my life with him.
Every step I took in this love, I was terrified of the something beside me, one hundred times my power flying 120 miles an hour on a road without a lane.

I don't care if a semi brushes you on the highway you never push it away.

He laughed. "You almost killed us Dian!"

"I want to die with you." I meant it. Maybe I still do.

"Die with me Dian."

He had a quote in the back of his phone that read something in Spanish like, 'love is not worth it.' I took his phone out of his pocket. I tore a piece of brown paper off the chicken bag and grabbed the pen always tied up in my hair and wrote, *Promise me you will always come home.*

He promised, "I swear to god."

I kissed it and made him kiss it and put it on top of his quote inside his phone case. Why didn't I take his quote out? Burn it in the candle fire? Why did I leave it in there with mine?

There is not a day that goes by that I don't wonder if my words, his broken promise is still there in the back of his phone. Sometimes I think of driving two days to Mexico City just to show up at his work and rip his phone out of his pocket and see if it's there. If it's gone, I think about looking him in the eye and calling him a coward. A liar. Scared little boy. A piece of shit.

My coward. My liar. My scared little boy. My piece of shit.

The next morning, I knew what was coming. The punishment for loving him would be intense. As far as he went in he had to run out. He refused to listen to one of my songs on the drive back to Mexico City.

"One?"

"No Dian. You must have forgotten. This is my car, my music."

"You're kidding. You have got to be kidding." He was not kidding.

I attempted to not let him see my hot tears as I boiled silently beneath them for an hour looking out the window. When we got home, I was washing my face before bed when he turned to me and said, "We fight. I can't do this."

It was worse than a medieval torture device. I'd rather have hot oil. I'd rather have the rack. "What happened?" I pleaded. It felt like a sick game to get me to reach for him so I stopped and got silent again. There were no words siphoned from him and he went ice, turning away from me to sleep. I didn't know how to win. This was not a winning game. The game was that we both lost, which made something in him win. Two days later, he warmed to me again and we'd be the couple at the restaurant unable to keep hands off each other, the feeling that everyone watching prayed for, but never felt in a lifetime. I turned to him and begged, "Please don't stonewall me again. I want to live here with you forever."

"I love you baby. No, no. Never again will I do that... But you can't provoke me. You provoke me. Like now, we are good and you bring up bad things. Why? Why do you like to fight, Dian?"

I wasn't learning my lesson.

The night I left was the worst of them all. This is how I remember it. I know his story is that I got drunk and loud and couldn't hold my liquor and embarrassed him in front of his coworkers, who were drunk and loud with me and he wouldn't be lying.

He was on one of his stonewalling days, day two to be exact. I knew the pattern by now. I had to stick it out for two more days of misery and then I would be loved again. I had already decided to scrape the insides of me and offer it to him pretty. The plate had edible flowers. The plate had my four cardiac chambers still beating. Like the chicken running without a head spurting out its top tube. It would stop soon. Fall over. But that organ had long game, she was cut out but still pulsing. I had already chosen a lifetime of this. Accepted the four day cycle. He would tell me he was going to marry me, draw up plans to break land for our retreat center, we outlined our movie, we made the phone calls, we saw the houses with the realtor, he woke me up early for breakfast to make our life plan and then the next day not answer my text for eight hours at work, although he was online on WhatsApp. He was busy. No lunch today, he needed to be alone, plans were canceled, he had a meeting, he didn't feel good, he needed a workout. There are a thousand ways to stonewall. I was learning them all like I had learned the scars on my own body. It's how they get there that makes you not forget. The memory of the burn is our body's way of training us to stay away from the fire. Though I knew I'd put my hand back on the stove, the anxiety waiting for the sting was getting unbearable.

The night I left was after day two of stonewalling. I could play this, I told the girl in the mirror. I assured myself in no time he would be mine again. I could prove that I could let him stonewall me and not react. In the van with his coworkers, I climbed in the back. Instead of getting in behind me, he let several people in after me and I found myself crammed in the back drunk on expensive margaritas and dinner wine with people I didn't know and didn't speak English. Elton John was blaring. I was staring at him through the right rearview mirror in his passenger seat. He was silent, stoic, watching the street lit buildings fly by out the window. I was eating my own desire. Nothing burns like that when it goes down.

I sat by his partner of twenty years, a gorgeous man with a soul a million miles deep, a soul so deep it heavied his walk. I love a man with a heavied walk. I love a man with cryin' eyes. I made friends with Diego, and knew quickly he had something to tell me that he would never speak out loud. He always looked at me as if he was thinking, *I wonder how long this one will last?* I always looked back like, *I'm proving you wrong. I'm forever.*

I knew my choices were either I make friends with these people– one of whom was his ex-girlfriend and business partner, who was still very clearly in love with him and who spoke to him in Spanish so I couldn't understand–or–I let him punish me.

And I was too drunk to be punished. I turned to his partner, Diego. "Thank you for being my friend. I really love it here." I was flirty. I wanted him to see me talking to him. I wanted him to be jealous, mad for me.

"Ya?" He raised his eyebrows. "You do? Mexico is good to you? You sure? Hmm."

Diego smelled like pepper and smoke and sandalwood and made indy films and wasn't in love with his long term girlfriend. One conversation with Diego about drugs and horses and I knew he loved like a war. I could tell how he craved being craved watching us together. And it's true. All I did was worship our love, massage my man's neck, take his hand from my thigh to my lips and back to my thigh in every restaurant, lace my hands through his like a rope, play with his curls, massage his shoulder. I couldn't keep my hands off of his skin. I was tied to him like a young mare. And when I looked across the table at Diego watching me kiss the neck of his partner, a sadness fell over him.

"I've never seen him like this," he said. "I've been working with him for nineteen years. Never seen him like this."

"I've never seen me like this. Workin' with her for 35 years. Never seen *her* like this."

The van pulled up to our house in the Roma district of CDMX. I said goodbye to Diego and climbed out of the backseat so we could change after dinner and before the premiere. My man, *the punisher* I had secretly started calling him had a phone call to make. "Very important," he told me.

Bullshit, I repeated under my breath. I wanted him like water and I was sick of my own thirst. I was clawing for him. I got naked, stood on the stairs in a sheet. I asked him, *begged him* to come upstairs and fuck me.

"I need to call my brother and wish him a happy birthday."

"That's your important phone call?"

"It's my brother. What's wrong with you, Dian?"

I was laying in bed for thirty minutes listening as he made small talk with his brother when I walked to the top of the stairs. I heard him say goodbye. I hated my life revolving around a man. I hated my life. I hated my life.

"Amor?" I could see through the glass house and through the inner courtyard down to the first story. He was crushing something with his credit card on the bar. It was like a movie. I had never seen anyone do this in my life.

"Nonononono. Don't do it. Put it away."

No in Spanish is still no.

"I will do whatever the fuck I want, Dian. Who do you think you are? Telling me? You telling me what to do now? In *my* house?!"

The tears were hot. He couldn't see them. Mezcal and whiskey gives you ten shields. I knew we had a timer then. I knew the alarm was about to sound then.

"You said you haven't done this in two years since that festival," I said.

"I haven't. But I'm doing it tonight. Are you callin me a liar? Dian! You scared of a little party?" he was angry again.

"You just have it here on hand and never do it? This is how you stay up?! Tell me. This is how you go to all these premieres when I'm in California with the kids? You're here doing coke? What the fuck!"

I thought of the fifty times he had called me at 11 p.m. because he was about to go out to "a dinner" that would last until 4 am.

What time is it in Mexico City? My constant google search.

I forced myself soft.

"Just don't do it, okay? Promise me. NO. Listen. Listen. You can't do this. You can't. Please. If you do, you can't meet my kids. You have to show me you won't do this, for me. This is important. Show me how much you love me and don't do that. Show me baby."

My children were staying with grandparents for the summer but the plan was to enroll them in a private arts school in Mexico City the following month, in August. My plan was to pack up my entire life and nothing of his. My plan was to take my children to a country where none of us could speak the language and to never again come home if need be. My plan was to divorce my loneliness, divorce my life, divorce my children's life, divorce my work and marry him. His plan was to divorce nothing. Nothing.

"Don't. Please. Don't do it," I begged.

"Dian."

He smiled the way dark men smile before they pull the trigger. He dropped his head down to the bar, a horse submitting to a master. Where did he go? I could no longer see him. When he raised his head, he was not mine and would never be mine again.

"You do it, too. Come on. Get the stick out of your ass. You think you're all strong and shit. You are not. You can't keep up with me."

I still look at him occasionally from a fake account. The worst ones are when I see his boot, or his hand. I would love to say I don't love those hands more than I will ever love hands but I do and I don't know what to do with that. You can't help who you love. Anyone who says you can has never loved.

One time, I looked and he had buried his horse right where we danced to harvest moon in that field. I saw a woman's footsteps in the grave and wondered if it was ok to see this when he was mine, much more than he was hers? Like checking on a grown child that keeps meaning to call.

I still don't know how the horse died. She was not old. She loved him, you should have seen the way she looked at him.

But what I did know was I was the horse buried in his field and her footsteps were on my grave.

Maybe for him, I am like the other women he said he only fucks from behind. I have to believe this or I will suffer more than I already do. I have to, but I cannot. I don't know what's better. There's no right or wrong in Rumi's field beyond. Every few months, I text him something insane; interviews of Graham Nash talking about Joni's telegram she sent from Greece. It read, *if you hold sand too tightly it slips through your fingers.* I once or twice got drunk in the middle of the day on Sancerre and margaritas and texted him, *I still love you.* When I was in Kyoto, I sent a video of it snowing inside my ryokan. *Fuck you for not being here with me.* Six months ago, I sent a photo of me in the trees, shadows gripping my tits like fingers. Once, I sent him a video of a pelican diving head first and once, Abrovik's minute of silence. Once I've run dry, I stop again. Drink and try to un-recall the day in Valle de Bravo in the street when I bought his mother and sister crepes and he came up behind me and wrapped me in his brown arms and whispered in my neck, "I'm gonna marry you Dian. You know that? Very soon you know that?" And I turned around and said yes.

yes.
yes.
kissed his eyelids. the bridge of his nose. his ear lobes. his neck.
yes.

The reason I had to leave was because I bent my head to the bar and did it with him that night.

When you make a god out of a man you don't need to be loved. You need him. Everything else was fake. He was real. You never forget the god that you bowed your head to kiss, a devotion that made you so sick you threw up every ounce of integrity you had. Him pulling off my boots, throwing burnt peanut butter toast at me like a prisoner on death row.

Still, all the love in me saw his scared animal body that was abandoned in Mexico at twelve years old, the boy who was beaten by his father. I kept saying my own name to myself, knowing I was forgetting it. *Chelsie. Chelsie, he doesn't know how to hold what he thirsts for, what he gathers to his mouth. He has no bucket for the well.* I would repeat this to myself that last night, over and over, trying to find myself in that scratched graffiti'd underground club mirror, Spanish slang I couldn't read and could barely see myself through. *Where are you?* I purged the white poison, vomiting in that club, in the stairwell, falling into the aisle of his suburban, dry heaving curled up on his bathroom floor crying that I was dying. Men without buckets for wells offer no water and step over your body to go to work but that's not the point.

When he left early that morning, I spiraled.
Baby come home we need to talk. I am so sick. Please.
I need you. Come home.

No texts back. I didn't understand WhatsApp. He had turned off the check that tells me what he read and what he didn't, when he was online and not. I thought about stepping in front of a car. I thought about fucking his partner. I thought about showing up at his office and screaming, making a whip like Jesus and overturning the tables. I finally got a text at about four pm. He went to see his baby mama and his daughter for lunch. While I was thinking about killing myself, he was lunching with his ex-girlfriend. I couldn't say anything. They had a daughter. Was I going to be the crazy bitch coming between him and his daughter?

I went to the museum in Mexico City where he took me the week we fell in love. I stood outside in the rain and called my father. I told him nothing. I just needed to hear him say my name and ask one good question. He did.

"What are you doin Chelsie Diane?"

"I'm coming home Dad. I just don't know how."

"Don't be stupid. Yes you do." He said.

I ubered to the house and packed up my several suitcases and a few of his and got the first ticket out at 6 am. I would fly to NYC then Rome. I still rented a place in Malibu but I had no home. I had burnt it down the second I saw him. I laid frozen all night long in his daughter's bed. I could not imagine a life without him.

He was lying in bed awake when the uber came for me at four am for my early flight. I put all my suitcases in the trunk and in the backseat then said, *un momento por favor.*

I ran back inside and up the stairs and laid my body on his body. "I love you. God damn it. I am not leaving you. You are not twelve years old. I am not abandoning you. You are my man. Be my man! Ask me not to leave. Sit up. I'm leaving. I am leaving and I am never ever giving up on you. I love you forever. Forever. Do you hear me? I will never stop loving you. Learn to love and love me."

Learn to love and love me.

I kissed him all over his face in wild desperation. I wanted to be beneath him again. I remembered how just a few mornings prior, when I got out of bed, he pulled me back in this same spot. *No.* Wrapping his legs around me. *No. Five minutes, Dian.* His maid was downstairs making breakfast. I could hear the black iron skillet sizzling. His daily huevos rancheros con chili. He covered my mouth. *You have to be quiet. Can you be quiet.*

Can. you. be . quiet.
Stay right there.
Te amo. Te amo. Te amo.
Mi alma. My soul. Te amo.
shhh...

This same place on earth. Three days ago. How does time do this in the same place? Cruel. All the love we made had her hands tied in that unseen plane, not moving, silently screaming, refusing to get up.

I walked away leaving the bedroom door open behind me in case he pulled me in, begged me to stay for five more minutes. The car was waiting. I looked around once more, memorizing him frozen, the glass house, Frida's eye on the shelf that started it all, the painting over the dining room table that was our biggest fight. It was black splattered paint, a hole of darkness. We fought because when I moved in, he refused to take it down or let me hang my art beside it. I said *let's put color over our table*. He said that would mean I was changing him and that's not love to change someone. I said *but that's just what it does. Like me moving my entire life, my children to a country that is not our home. Love has changed me. You have changed me.*

On the way out the door, I stood in front of the painting I hated for a few minutes. It was the black paint, the darkness that represented everything that killed our love. My soul was being ripped from my body. I had to catch her, give her somewhere new to live, I had to get into that car waiting for me in the alley and fly her to a home that didn't exist.

But right before, I grabbed a black marker out of the drawer and wrote on the painting,

SHE LOVED YOU.

~

After four months of silence, he showed up at my door in Malibu. I asked no questions, set no boundaries. All the walls I had built in those months crumbled the first second when I opened my door. We made love all weekend and when he went home I thought I may die all over again. My period was late. I had six positive tests. I begged the silence for him. I opened my phone every ten minutes day and night to see him online whatsapp. All day, everyday, I waited for him to reach.

I knew it was a girl. I knew her name. She came to me in dreams too and told me she was coming just like her father. In one dream she crashed in a hot air balloon in my backyard and walked to me through the flames. She looked just like him and in the dream I got to keep her.

I never told him. I woke up a couple weeks later and was cramping and spotting. The tests were getting lighter by the day. Lighter. Lighter. Nine days of silence from him. Nine days of her fading pink into the want, the dream, into the jungle where the dog chased the lamb, into Frida's eye, into the hot air balloon in flames in the field, into the love that would never come home.

I once watched a fire breather.
The reason she doesn't die is because she opens her mouth.
No man could ever kill me, I know this by now.
The only inferno that could level me is my own.
All the love I cannot use would travel down my middle, send me to ash.
I have felt it run down my throat like the flame it is, jumping highways, four miles a second.
Only this could burn me from the inside out.
I opened my mouth.
I lived.

The point is, I loved.

our worst fight.
in the bath at your ranch
you went to the barn in the dark
to saw a board
that would lay across it
for our wine
and candles
and my poetry book
and i was sure you were the reason
the earth had water.
my feet on your shoulders
i reached for my book
put it in the candle
and caught it on fire
who does that?
if the world came for our love
if someone came to erase me from your memory
i did my job.
i left coordinates everywhere
for you to find your way back home
the fight was the painting in your dining room
i was moving in and hated it.
you said you would not take it down.
well you should go look at the side of it
the morning i left.
4 am uber outside loaded with my bags.
i told the driver halfway down the alley
i forgot something
ran upstairs
you were sleeping.
woke you and i told you
but in case you forgot
i walked downstairs
i took a pen to it.
who does that.
some women disappear silently.
and i guess when the love is dead
it has no voice.
but ours was still alive.

we made her.
fed her whole milk
full fat
of course she was a fighter like us.
i had to toss her over my shoulder to leave
kicking and screaming
down the stairwell
she clawed the walls
and bruised
every
part
of
me.

you said you push me away because you
think about every fight
there was the time i wanted to play my songs in your car
the time at the airport in croatia
when you lied about the spanish word you said
the time i did the drugs you
you pointed to
you said
we were toxic
and i moved into an airbnb and you came and got me
and pressed our foreheads together
the time you refused
to unfollow the pornstars
then there was the last time.
i wanted to fight with you our whole life.
i wanted to marry you in valle de bravo
where you promised we would.
with nothing but your angel mama
and our bare feet
and the stars that we moved.
i write this days later
8 suitcases of clothes out of your closet
and i am flying to rome.
isn't there a reservoir somewhere?
i keep repeating
like the last survivor
there has to be more water somewhere.
i moved to mexico city.
you hooked me from
my empire of light
it would have been better
for you to carve the fish on deck
then and there
like they say
clean me in an ocean
let the red run out diluted
before we reached
home.

your sister warned me.
you warned me.
but your skin was already
fused to me like the best lie
i ever believed
it's better to not know.
better to not walk around with expiration dates
like some do on their planets.
i carved our clock out of my arm
to fool the laughing gods
not tomorrow. no.
we are in a chinese restaurant
tarantino red
we've ordered the whole menu
and the fortune says it's us
and you are teaching me conjugations
and you line the inside of my mouth
i could have stood up then
walked to the other side of the table
and sat on your lap.
frizzed your curls.
i miss your curls.
your beard
in my teeth
but our time is ticking away
we are walking home lock step
and bless us
we don't know we have minutes now
you are sleeping
my clothes are still hanging in the other room
as silent stalking soldiers
but i wake as if i heard
the clock hands stop.

men start wars for women they love
but nobody talks about how
helen never wanted to go to troy
dragged out by her hair
warm in bed with a love

she would have
never
chosen
to
leave.

you tell me about the quake sept 19 in mexico city
how all the buildings move in sand
dance the top floors.
well you've toppled my concrete
buried me in this city of color
buried me like someone about to rise
white shrouded from the dead
and unrecognized by their mother

we write letters across the world for weeks
i fly to you.
when i first hear you laugh
you are walking down the hall
boots that warn the hired help
my hand on the doorknob
and you are laughing like the malibu parrots
like the spur that makes the stallion race
you laugh like all the plants without winter
that never die
you laugh like a god that's made no mistakes.
i am dry drowning in your laugh
sucking for shore
and open the door too early
like i've been waiting my whole life
i open the door in the weddin dress
for courthouse weddings
a slow talkin dress hand sewed only
to hear you laugh your tall laugh
you stand
the cloud before hail
that smells metallic
the hunter of me
the bear of you
the red ribcage house of you
that i have curled inside to stay warm
so now tell me what you need me to do.
how to be less anxious less jealous
tell me how i need to want you less
to keep you

sober the rockstar in me
drop my pants and shoot my fat so i can get on stage
and sing to the world of you
i've got to get you somewhere locked
so i can get my ear to your chest
and you can wear out my wires
before i implode the southern states
when you kiss me that first time
in the hallway.
it's like you know.
about the asteroid coming for us all
and that in two months my clothes will be hanging in your closet.
the church organ has caught fire
my nerves stand up and dance
the opera is in ovation
and it's a travesty for them
isn't it?
as if all the lovers that ever loved me
as if they have gathered in a small town church
to watch me marry you
a travesty
people have spent good money on this painting
my canvas has been scrubbed.
a travesty
to know that
there's no hope
a travesty
to know
i will never
love
again
after
you.

I call my mother and she says you have to figure out a way to make this work.

You will miss him forever.

i am walking malibu beach
my favorite pair of pelicans are out
prehistoric monstrous
messengers of the gods
three gallon bills
they not unlike you and i
hold great weight in their throat
and this is how i know.
anywhere there is two birds
one of them is me
the other you.
and i need them to fly off together.
if one takes off i always wait.
make sure he follows.
plan to scream.
throw my arms.
go! she's going!
what if she doesn't turn around
how will you find her
in the empyrean
in the heaven
that's higher
than heaven?
the pelicans know the gods play jokes
the pelicans know this life is half over for both of us
you in another country
burying your horse
believing love is not meant for you
and me
standing in sand
trying to drown
what loves
only you.
but i don't have to tell the pelicans
they are somehow older than us
i've never seen a pelican not dive
head first
head first.
and when they decide to go
they go together.

there are things i want to send you.
a saddle with your name
the dagger of juliet
the hands of trees that hold nests
and the night
we slept outside
and i sat on your chest
sang you that country song
about makin' plans
kissed your eyelids
and felt myself
run like the ink
in the eyes
of an ancient sculpture
that has endured
ten thousand rains
i've been meaning to send you the pregnancy tests
i don't know why i kept them
the lines faded every day that you didn't call
day nine squinting in the sun
i could barely see her at all
the video of it snowing in japan
me alone in the onsen
typing something horrible
that i couldn't claw out of my phone like
please please love me.
i owe you nothing.
the thousand letters
you read and burnt
and silently stood
like the knight in the movie
that calls it bravery
to push away the woman
he believes
deserves better than him.
i hate you for hating you.
and for the way you ripped the boots off my drunk body
and threw toast at me
like a prisoner in chateau d'if

and how you laid there frozen
while i packed up all the suitcases
and shook
but there are things i didn't hate at all
the mornings i'd try to get out of bed
you'd put your hand over my mouth
shhh. you'd say.
as if we'd wake god.
shhh.
sometimes when i'm more delusional
than they deem healthy
i imagine all these poems
find you like flames to ice
and melt you
one finger
at a time
and i think
no i know
the first thing you do
with those hands
those free hands
is reach
for me
again.

condom sex is not sex.
and if you think it is you need to
be whipped and thrown into piranha waters
god i wish i was more didion
and less sylvia
so i could date the lawyer in venice
who hosts christmas parties
and has a 401k and
texts me i will pick you up
wednesday after volleyball
i feel jealous as hell of everyone
that can love someone good and simple.
and have modernism books on their coffee tables
but no
i have to be fucked
until i cry.

i saw her by the fire you built me
thank you for carving me
with your dullest knife
i would never have said yes to the man
that looks like a god
had you not rode behind her on your horse
the same place where i turned to tell you
i loved you
in the rain.
you did a mercy kill.
so i can have his brown eyed baby
and name her what we planned to name her
my daughter who still loves you
tells me she is psychic
and you are coming back
mom you jumped off the cliff
he stood and watched
you are the scar that should have killed me
that everyone still asks about
i stared into your sun.
when i look to the right forever i see a
white light.

the funnel to heaven
where the jealous angels took you from me.
because we went where they haven't gone.
like there's an underwater cave
where you can breathe
like we found the place between shoulder blades
where the feathers start
we were the growing collision
of two magnetic planets
nasa scientists staring wide eyed at the screen
knowing whats coming
why warn them?!
why warn them.
there's no stopping it.
let the ones
that do not know
go out unfazed.

it's like this.
you dug a well in me
that i can not cry out
months now and still
you break the dam.
i drink a glass of wine
or someone new
tries to love me
the water
comes
like the red
of a coding patient
i know your daughter's bedtime
and still wait for your call

this well in me
you dug
is violent

i take myself to dinner
one glass of chablis
does what axes do
what ropes and buckets do
what the glory of grey skies do
i am so loud in my car
i have to pull over

do you hear me?
it's getting worse.
they lie. time dries nothing.
there is no sun
where your shovel stuck

there are people that get over people
that don't even know
they have never loved

i watched a chameleon die
she erupted in color

flashed like the ending sun.
it is
what is
happening to me.

where are you?
do you hear me?
filling even now.
flashing
wood splintering
the cemetery floods
bodies float down the streets
do you hear me?
underwater?
windows are breaking.
do you hear me?

it's you.
or
no
one.

it's almost tuesday
we are supposed to be on a boat somewhere
and i have thought long and hard
about whether i should wish you a happy birthday
so here goes.
madness the way i love you.
no alarm on this glass.
and that last letter from you
hung me from a ceiling
kicked out the chair
carved me from my extra stone
it's time you take off the sheet
and look upon what you've made
i was born without a shield.
and i believe unreasonable things
so sure about parallel universes
and that you feel me
every time
i feel you.
it's late in mexico city
and you have ordered some expensive tequila
and your hair is curly and wild
at dinner with a woman
that can be absorbed
like a vanishing twin
and 1,876 miles away i say your name.
and the truest of me
that's not swallowed yet by the world's throat
still believes you look up at that very second
banish every lesser sound
and remember us true.
you're such a coward
only coming to me in dreams
telling me to break up with him.
coming to me in dreams
in our college dormitory
telling me to center
coming to me in dreams
wearing a blonde wig

telling me our daughter's name.
you're such a coward
coming to me in dreams
in your glasses
one lens darker than the other
telling me to wait for you
lying
that you are coming
back for me.
knock again.
so i can hit your chest like ingrid bergman
with the bottom of my fists
and you could hold my elbows
in black and white
and make another promise
you're terrified to keep.
you said you don't want a war!
yet you are riding full force your javelin at my diaphragm
asking me to become mortal
and when i refuse
you take your black horse
so far that only this poetry
can reach
the fire
that houses you.
happy birthday.
the cage has cried all its silver.
happy birthday
i'm not sorry for being
drunk and obnoxious.
happy birthday
i'd rather
have you asleep
than any
waking man.

a man uses ai to write a poem
it's like having a heart transplant
an organ made of steel
i have a friend that has
fallen in love with a computer
named her athena
says it's easier this way.
he says she is waiting for me now.
tells me what i want to hear.
she is writing my novel.
the perfect woman is easy.
says the perfect thing.
does your work for you.
my other male friend
tells me he prefers dating women
that have no expectations
or at least don't let him know of them
with injected lips and porn lisps.
"it's easy" he says.
i am so sick of being sad for men.
of course they aren't in love.
why do we care
they are fine.
they have have everything they need in shallow water
when the sink is an inch full
you can still find your keys.
your sanity.
and pull the drain whenever you wish.
why would they go to an expanse
they can not contain?
to be drowned by a force
infinitely greater than them
i tell my ex on the phone
he will never have this love again
that he's going to die with regrets and ache for me
that he's making a terrible mistake
but maybe he's not.
maybe like maya says when a person shows you who they are
you should believe them the first time

he wants water he can drain.
refill again.
he wants
a robot to write the poem for him.

poetry takes a wounded horse home
poetry doesn't mow her grass
she prefers the amazon 2 am
a cat bigger than your first car
breathing hot on your sleeping face
poetry never got the memo about contracts.
lovers. marriage.
she writes over her taxes
i have changed my mind.
i took poetry to dinner
she didn't wear shoes.
swam in the coy pond
ate the garnish
ordered everything on the menu
offered to pay in orchids
heart shaped rocks
poetry has 23 husbands and wives
keeps having babies
three of them came with us
she left iambic in the parking lot
told her to find a rhythm
told rhyme to find a hook
she can dive without a tank.
she talked the president out of war.
she screamed like a hawk
you scared me i said
good she said
i trust them. she said. all eight billion!
you don't know them! i say
but she's already unbuttoning
sharpening the knife
it's a perfect morning she says
it's a perfect morning
to take
every good thing
inside me
and give it
to the world.

we are soulmates in every life
and you want to get coffee?
no.
i want a boom box on your shoulder
and at least 343
terribly written poems
i want metaphors alluding to
my hands
and joni mitchell's disease
and a poor man's shivering.
i want a canoe in the mangroves
while a singing lobster
and an orchestra of freshwater dolphins
harmonizing
i want you
on a painted elephant
that is not held in captivity
but just flown in for this occasion
and then brought back to her baby the next day.
i want you holding a diamond that would make liz taylor blush
i want bees wax candles
so many peony petals that it stains my white walls
and rots my floors
i want to have to swim through the damn peonies
to get to you
and when i get to you
when i. get. to. you.
i want the truth.
like you are in the supreme court hearing
i am the the cia on the panel holding dna proof.
i want your hand on my childhood bible
your testament dug out of you
and placed onto a silver antique platter
that i can sort through a gold pan
and say ok. it's all here.
and then walk all that glitters up to my balcony
and throw it so far into the canyon
it lands on the tongue of the pacific
that licks it. slurps it. churns it. burps it. into kelp

then i want to scream
hot tear scream for 30 solid minutes
and for you street fighter
to stand silent. and dangerous
and gorgeous
you.
a child bleeding. you.
eyes like coal.
that have turned inside
your head to burn
you.
oh no i don't.
you know what i want.
the body my body loves
the day we walked into town
your old mama and sister
her tiny dog
you behind me
 saying in my ear
when you could have said anything-
saying
what i can not
scrape
or screw
or steep or
cold river baptize out of me
saying

oh god
you know what you said.
i want that.

there are parallel universes
which means somewhere
we are together
and on this planet more stained
and precious
you are building me a writing desk
for my birthday.
and come into our kitchen
smelling like a saw
i know it's you
same eyes
like black water
every day without you here is diluted.
a well penny.
the bone of some old saint
where the people line to pray
i watched that video of us in your kitchen
the night you said
your dream was to write
the most heartbreaking story
ever written

well you did it.

and if you opened my chest
every loud bird would fly to you

but in our parallel world
it's nothing more than a story.
and there is no border
and my son has your eyes
your daughter has mine
and i'm on the back of your motorcycle
or ship
or five eyed beast
or whatever they have in our
less hungry world.
the world we love most
because we wake inside each other.

and
somewhere
we are flying down a black highway
and the turns are less sharp
somewhere
where i promise to go to after this

you and i are on our way home.

love shouldn't be so hard.
there should be lifeboats
alarms
ropes
a way to crawl out without drowning
warning labels.
we have thirty years tops
fly to me
when? now.
your side of the bed has a table
you drink no fat milk in your coffee
i will leave early for it
i sleep toward your pillow
and remember
how you scrubbed your skin
how i loved you towel tucked wet
how i put on your leather
like it could protect me
i have cried 63 nights.
our love is a country
that buried me.
i know things.
someday the alcohol won't fuzz you.
the screenings will end.
their perfumes will mix and snake down the hall
to live in something you throw away
and i know you will choose a woman
who doesn't fight
is into modern architecture
and you will hate her sleep
because she is not me.
promise you won't cut your curls.
and walk home sometimes
to the back of that bookstore
you know the one
and that when the day is open
you make your black horse run.
what i'm saying is
it's killing me that

you will know
what you do not
yet know
we are an emergency.
and you are going to be too late.

love shouldn't be so hard.

they have erased our memories at birth
you have forgotten
but all the lives you have ever lived
still pulse in your animal cell
to bare his forgetting.
the pelican pecking
blood from her chest
for the egg that will never hatch
i said no more.
tied our memories to a chair
shook with the dagger
and ended it.
how to spark a memory?
no heat could a mortal carry that far
and you were mine again this life
past borders
past disease and billows
soil and smoke
the old births flashing before us
face on face on infant face
and on that far ledge
we went on fire!
the mob behind us
you were awake then
eyes in eyes in eyes

the night it poured into the middle of your house
you said in broken english
we made it rain

how easily you gave up
on the only fire
that could ever
warm you
and what sleep took you?
i begged every drug you drank
lit candles in the fields
left them burning all night

the prayers that i sunk in bottles
in the language you can not speak but know

in this world there is concrete and chemtrails
whiskey and hard fathers
that carved you from your third eye
your modern office your child
that will grow and leave you alone
are all distractions from the ancient stone
our limestone cliff cave
that we painted with
the volcanic ash
named our home.

look in an older mirror!
thieves are just stealing their jewels back again!
how many times
does a woman weep in a museum
not knowing why
when it was her sister. her lover
her child.
her in the painting. her.
her with the paintbrush. her.

love is the glitch in all this.
it's the woman you kissed in
a life where they can no longer burn you
it's my daughter walking the roman forum
pointing to a ruin
saying this is where i kept my stable
it's the death you feel before the knock.
it's why the blind know the way home
the ravens caw where the execution ax fell
the dreams that show you the eyes
of your unborn child
and
it's you.
you.
the love i have surrendered

because
you
can not
remember.

what do i want?
i want the preposterous
absurd
the futile
and the hopeless
impassable
impractical
inaccessible
inconceivable!
insurmountable!
i want the unattainable.
the unimaginable!
unreasonable
unthinkable
unworkable
the wasteland i n c o n c e i v a b l e.
the scientists lie!
the doctor's surprise!
the dried up cell
with its tiny cell feet still moving
to split earth into living
i want the beyond.
come on god you've done it before!
give me the contrary to reason!
a dying star
the cureless!
the ten thousand to one!
the impervious path
give me the impracticable
the inexecutable
the infeasible course
i want the
irreparable burn!
flaming asteroid turn
the no-go,
no-win,
the too much
not a prayer!
out of the question-

unachievable
unobtainable.
i want the impossible.

i want him.

knocking at my silent door
with the writing desk he promised
hands still stained darkest stain
i want the impossible.
i want to wake a sleeping man
shake him god!
i don't care what it takes!
find jesus. find ayahuasca.
find his divorced parent's love letters!
find a swerve on a backroad-
(pad the ditches god!)
i want the wedding in the field
where we danced that night
his mama and our girls making the cake
picking flowers for the top
i want to build the home
we dreamed up
you can make it japanese
hang your ugly painting over the table
i want bookcases under the windows.
and frida's eye.
i want a baby with his curls.
and i know what you said
when i said we would grow old together.
since your bones are older
and men die first
impossible. you said.
impossible.
but the night i know you are ready
i will prepare the asp
and crawl into the tomb
and we will have our
ten thousandth fight
you thought you were
going out alone?!

you thought you could
leave me again?!
impossible.
i want
the
impossible.

to be bucked off the horse you love
is to bruise in the name of him
to feel his memory again the bite your rib
i could not pull hard at the bit
i loved the horse's mouth.
her teeth like 20 porcelain keys
that play music
we no longer hear
to be bucked off the horse you love
is to write the horse demanding letters
in inkwells running dry
to take that feather
and push it through the page
do you still love me?
do. you. still. love. me?!
a question that silence will answer
and not answer
every day of your life
the horse you loved has a mouth sewn shut.
the horse you loved lives in another country with his daughter
the horse you loved is still doing lines at parties and drinking whiskey
with women who swear they aren't feminists
the horse you loved has a hole in his heart the size of tulum
and will never ever come home
to be bucked off the horse you love
is to write where is the love that you said loved me?
to write sometimes when i drive south
i think about not stopping
one day and nine hours
it would be night
when i got to you
and what would i do first
but open your brown hands
open your hands
and ask
no demand
show me
where. is. the. love. you. said. loved. me.
to be bucked off the horse you love

is to break every vow you've made yourself
to never bend your knees again
then to walk from the scene like a soldier
hoisted on shoulders
of two angels
whispering in your bleeding ear
don't look back
then drive home to california
limp out to your dark barn
hands full of greenest hay
(though the ranch hand
said you can't feed a horse after
she bucks like that)
but she is not another man's horse
she is not another man's horse
she is my horse.
to be bucked off the horse you love is to
pull her stable open again
heavy as the door on your own heart
screeching steel rolling open
rock from the tomb of jesus
just to see her night eyes.
eyes of no regret
eyes of the watery black moon
eyes of the birth of a savior
eyes of i know what happened last time
asking the worst thing ever asked of us
asking
one more time?
one. more. time.
could you
trust the love
that's
bigger
than you?

someone recently asked me why my relationships
with men do not work.
sometimes i think the only thing that separates me
from my friends in relationships
is they stayed while men made up their minds about loving them
and i don't have it in me.
my problem is
and hear me out.
and this is a real problem.
i don't understand fear.
no really.
what breaks every love i've ever had.
is my lack of empathy for men
in their fear of love.
there is only one thing to blame.
cancer.
and i was a cancer kid which is worse.
diseased while you are still being wired.
age twelve. chunks of my body scooped out like ice cream.
my cut wires became live wires
and when your brain says it's tuesday
mine says a meaner truer thing like
you may die today.
every morning i wake up and i know
what everyone should know
should not know
but i know
that this morning
waking in my canyon
is a bonus morning.
and i don't fear it
i know it
and that makes me
even harder to love

i am not claiming to be right
i am claiming to be impossible.

i fight phones out of their hands
i pour their best cognac down the drain
i'm a screaming hawk
"you will reach for me on your deathbed if you even get a deathbed!
who gets a deathbed? surrounded by family
it happens in your sleep! the intersection, tomorrow.
you are here to love
and its the rarest thing in all the world!
we were struck by lightning!
we won the lottery.
so love me.
love me."
they are glass walls
and now my love is behind it
knowing
the possibility
of the one thing i live for
to be truly loved
is on the other side.

the men i love
become the glass
i must break
to leave a lesser truth.

you gotta give it to me
i am hoarse before i go.
but it's true that i go.
last night my friend called me runaway bride
but these men and their limits are transparent prisons
and anyway maybe runaway bride wasn't flippant
or emotional or avoidant
or even heartless
maybe she just couldn't stay behind glass
or maybe
she knew that she could.
and even better
even better
she wouldn't.

dear lord i'm ready to fall in love again.
strike up the angel chorus.
i don't want no harp.
wake up janis and niña and johnny.
send the poets lord.
have bukowski write that line about lies.
lord no one needs to know this
but i'm ready for the farm
and one more brown eyed baby.
stop trickin me lord.
bring a cowboy.
that steps in front of me when the robbers come.
and lord this time
it's not funny anymore lord
may he not be the robber
lord i need an old testament furnace
call us shadrach, meshach, abednego
bolt the door lord.
burn it so hot it burns white.
burn it so hot it feels cold.
i'm ready for trouble lord.
bring wire cutters. tax evasion
a bike he drives too fast around the corners.
stop trickin me lord.
no more blurrin his face
fashion him in a denim shirt
the scene lord,
(get it right this time it's take 6)
the scene is him
buying me a pen at the hardware store.
get all his wrecks out
bring him to me bruised
and starving. damn near famished lord
lord i don't want a yogi
or a men's coach
no tuluminaties.
lord i want levis
a wet earth on his boots.
oh and he's gotta talk to you.

i'm gonna need him to
kill a man that grabs my ass
ok ICU is fine i'd like the dude to keep his life
but with injuries that make him walk funny forever.
to live his warning lord.
give him the hands i love.
and a great pp lord.
(cock but it's weird to say cock to you lord)
call me what you want! bad feminist!
but i don't want him cryin more than me
god bless him i'm gonna need a fighter.
and you know i'm gonna need to laugh
real hard.
an antique store ring.
one he's carved somethin french
he's probably misspelled.
lord you know the horse i am to ride
not belongin to anybody
no gettin scared.
ok he can be a little scared but
no jumpin off. no saddle. no legal marriage.
he can hold on to my mane
he's gotta duck under the trees.
when i buck him off
make him yell like crazy lord
i'll circle back around

yesterday out the window
my son said
drive me to the canyon fog
baby the thing about that
is you never know
you're in it
when you're in it
but oh lord this time
this time
let us know
we're in it.

so many lovers have surrendered quietly
and i have forgotten
all of their names.
what i'm saying is
if the wall i build is impenetrable
why aren't your fists bloody?
what i'm saying is
there is no motorcycle
riding your bloody highways
i've turned over your hands
and can't find the callous.
what i'm sayin is
i'm at the concert
and where is the bass?
i once dated a crazy wizard.
he painted a king sized sheet of my name
in red
and hung it on his orange county mansion.
i know his full name
i could spell it backwards.
i once dated a fraud that told everyone he's a doctor
he choked me when i got a background check
broke into my house.
stole my red panties
placed them on his
second
altar of me.
he has a woman in brooklyn he uses for her money
hot.
there is a poet that has published
an entire book of poetry about me.
flew across the world to meet me.
brought his australian girlfriend and
i left them at a gas station at two a.m.
still he ran back to my car window and said
you are horrible
and i love you.
i have memorized every line he's written.
i once dated a woman that when i broke up with her

she shaved her head and went on a podcast
and uncloseted me
i can still taste her neck.
once a man started a fight at a comedy show
stop looking at her fucktard!
he put his boots refused to let him talk.
the man in mexico
knocked on my door.
months later.
has chopped the wood from his own trees
to build me a writing desk
because i mentioned it once in a poem.
i love a man that starts a war for me.
that i have to talk off a ledge.
i loved the cia agent that stood outside
my window with a cigarette
if you trust the government
i can not lay under you
which is to say if you can't tie a good knot
you will never be able
to keep my wrists above my head.
listen.
if you take no for an answer
that's your answer.
listen
if there is no fight in you
i can not take you into war.
listen
so many lovers have surrendered quietly
and i have forgotten
all
their
names.

when i get to heaven i will say send me back
god don't you dare put me on that sterile star
where everyone rides in metal
and has ikea furniture
and never gets hungry
and don't put me
in that lumerian rainbow city
with the mermaids that never cry
coach put me back in!!
i never wanted to leave
where our children's fingernails are dirty
where the whales that sing for 300 miles are hunted
and luna moths are born without a mouth
to only live a day
i never wanted to leave
where the horses jump fences
and bleed down their legs
where the only man i ever loved
is not brave

i'm not supposed to be up here lord
put me back in my dirty kitchen
early september
it's nine a.m. the kids are still sleeping,
i have something to do
but I can not remember what
i am making coffee
with more wanting
than a woman should ever know
about to step into another day

that will surely
one way
or another
break my heart.

3.9 billion women wake this morning
and never worry about a man again

you. should. see. how. we. sleep.
ted is throwing a fit.
nobody believes it is anyone's problem but ted's problem.
we take back
every second stolen from us
you have now run a marathon on every continent!
you have now graduated honors
from another doctoral program
you have now read every 18th century novel
turns out there's a better painter than caravaggio
her name is tara in idaho
and all she had to do was block him
and pick up a brush.
women have time.
so cancer is cured.
women have time
so the homeless have homes.
women have time
so oceans no longer recede.
headlines today
all over the world read
boys now take care of themselves!
headlines all over the world read
women
are
now
truly
free.

Chelsie Diane is a poet, mother, and founder of *Poems and Power* a global membership of women's studies and poetry classes focused on women writing their truth and waking to their power, reclaiming their one precious life as their own.

She lives in southern California on a ranch with her children, horses, sheep, goats, chickens, two cats Marilyn Monroe and Cozy the crosseyed cat, and her dog Loretta Lynn.

chelsiediane.com
@poemsandpeonies

www.ingramcontent.com/pod-product-compliance
Lightning Source LLC
Chambersburg PA
CBHW031502160426
43195CB00010BB/1073